FORGOTTEN HEROES

✧ ✧ ✧ ✧ ✧

by Michael Bentinck

www.michaelbentinck.com
MY DAD MY HERO.ISBN.0952 6157 11.
FORGOTTEN HEROES.   0952 6157 2X.
A WILL TO LIVE.   0952 6157 03.
WAR TIME WOMEN.   0952 6157 54.
WAVING GOODBYE.   0952 6157 62.
WAR TIME MEMORIES.   0952 6157 46.
TIMES NOT FORGOTTEN. Volume One.

CONTENTS

Published by Michael Bentinck © 1995

Typeset in 11pt ITC Garamond
and printed on environmentally-friendly paper
by Print-Out, Histon, Cambridge, UK

ISBN 0 9526157 2 X

ACKNOWLEDGEMENTS

My thanks go to all who buy this book, for without you I could not help my FORGOTTEN HEROES. To the six friends that I have made while writing their stories, and for the thousands more out there that I have heard from while writing this book. My thanks to Mr. Alastar MacBean, Mr. Ben Bingham and Mr. Stanley Chown MBE, for their kindness in sending me the photos and memorabilia to use in the book. My thanks to Mike Johnson and his team at Print-Out, my publishers, for their support and help in preparing the book with me. Last but not least to my wife Hilary without whose help I could not have got this book written, for while I was busy writing it, she was kept busy sending off all the books of "MY DAD MY HERO" to you our valued customers. She to has made so many new friends from amongst you all that she has asked me to send you all her best wishes. She has sat beside me in tears as she has opened and read your letters, and her heart goes out to you all (believe me she has a big heart for such a little person). It was her idea to make up the last chapter of this book from your letters.

My special thanks go to another of my HEROES, Mr. Ronald Searle, for his help and kindness in allowing me to use his illustrations from his wonderful book "TO THE KWAI AND BACK."

DEDICATION

This book is dedicated to all who suffered at the hands of the Japanese after the fall of Singapore in 1942 on the 15th February. Their freedom was taken from them on that day, for what they were to face for the next four years was to change their lives for ever – and not just for the men themselves, but also for their wives and their families. Life would never quite be the same again. For the men who were lucky enough to come home, (yes, I say lucky, for that is what they were) their lives could not be the same again, for they have to live on with those memories of the things they saw and had to do, like my dear late father. It broke many of them and many of them that are alive today are finding that the terrible memories are coming back to them, and are becoming a living nightmare.

Many of the men look quite well but as many of you will know, once the mind is tormented, your quality of life is gone. Many of these men are lucky enough to have their wives to care for them, but you can imagine the strain and stress it puts on them, for they too have had their share of suffering; many of them told me of those four years they suffered in those dark days of the forties, of not knowing where their husbands and sweethearts were, or if they were alive or dead; most of them received only one letter in those four years and some received no word at all, and many had young children to bring up on their own. I have received many letters from these children – many of them never knowing their father, as he had been killed in the action at the fall of Singapore or had died as a prisoner of war in some camp along the line of the death railway.

The sacrifice these men and their families have made for our today must never be allowed to be forgotten, I know how privileged I am to be allowed to tell these mens' stories, for I know that these men don't like to talk of what happened to them, perhaps they feel that with me being the son of one of them that I, too, am part of their story. My heart goes out to all these forgotten HEROES, for trusting me to tell their story for future generations to read about.

I shall never forget the time I spent with each of them in their own homes and the tears we shared together as we spoke of the horrific things they had all been through. As they said, they had been to hell and back. I pray that God will keep them safe and well to enjoy their twilight years for they have suffered enough. God bless them all.

Bert Grimes lays a wreath at Kranchi in memory of all the those brave men who didn't make it home.

INTRODUCTION

The book you are about to read is full of true stories, like my first book "MY DAD MY HERO" – the stories of what happened to men after the fall of Singapore to the Japanese, on February 15th 1942. These men just could not imagine what lay ahead of them over the next four years. They were to see and experience things that only those who were out there can really understand.

My time spent with these brave men has been an honour for me, to be able to hear their stories at first hand, I know is a great honour – for these men don't talk about what happened to them; perhaps it brings back too many horrific memories for them. It brought back to me the times my late father and I had sat and talked over things that he had suffered at the hands of the Japanese, when we would both end up in tears, for such is the heartfelt pain of suffering felt for these men that suffered for our today.

I know that many of these men feel forgotten and are even called the forgotten army, but perhaps now that some of them have told their stories for further generations to read, they will get the recognition they so richly deserve.

My thanks go out to all who buy this book, for you are helping me to help these men who are still suffering from tropical illness and mental torment some fifty years on.

Through the work of the Far Eastern Prisoners of War Association, Mr. Don Few, treasurer of the Cambridge YASUME Club in Auckland Rd., Cambridge, himself a prisoner of war at the hands of the Japanese, and worker on the death railway, helps the men who are still alive today that are suffering from tropical illness, get by day to day by helping get war pensions for them. I feel they all deserve a pension for what they did for our country and for our today, but I know enough to realise that any government will only help those in real need, and believe me many of these brave men that are still alive today need medical help, but many of them are to proud to ask for it, for they are of a different generation from us today.

If you feel you could help these men in any way please write to the Cambridge YASUME Club in Auckland Rd., Cambridge. But please know that you have already helped them a little bit by buying this book.

If you would like to meet some of these forgotten heroes, then take time to find your local FEPOW club, or your British Legion. Call in and have a quiet drink with them. I can assure you that you will be glad you did. Listen to what they have to say, and of how they feel about our country today, and I think like me you will find they have the answer to most of todays problems.

Mike and Hilary Bentinck with Eric Bullen, Bill Moody, Les Phillips and Don Few of the Cambridge Yasume Club, with a cheque for the Far Eastern Prisoners of War Association, raised by sales of Mike's first book MY DAD MY HERO.

(Courtesy Cambridge Newspapers Ltd.)

Newspaper headlines reflect the problems in Singapore in 1942.

(Courtesy Cambridge Newspapers Ltd.)

Chapter One

JIM BENTINCK'S STORIES

Jim Bentinck, as many of you will know, was my late father and many of you will have read his true story in my first book "MY DAD MY HERO". It is from the success of that book that I have been encouraged to write this book of true stories, and I knew I could not leave out two stories that my dear father shared with me, as he lay ill in Ely R.A.F. Hospital. I left them out of my first book as I felt they were horrific and too sad to write about, but many of the men I have met while researching this book have confirmed to me that the two stories are true, and so I share them with you now.

Jim Bentinck was in the 1st battalion of the Cambridgeshire Regiment – many of the other Regiments called them the Fen Tigers. He was wounded in action and left for dead, but he was lucky enough to be picked up by some retreating Australian army soldiers, who got him to hospital where the doctors saved his life. Many of you will have read what happened to him in Alexandra hospital and know how lucky he was to survive the bloody massacre there as told in my first book. He was sent from there after the fall of Singapore to Changi prison, before being moved on to River Valley Camp on the outskirts of Singapore, where he was informed he had to drive the Japanese executioner around and if he did not do as he was told he would be put to death himself. He was a young man of twenty years old and the things he saw and had to do gave him nightmares for the rest of his life, and it was while he was ill in hospital at Ely he shared these two stories with me. As many of you will know, when he died I found photographs of him with the executioner and some of the horrific things he was witness to at this time. He told me how he buried over two thousand bodies in the mass grave on the outskirts of River Valley Camp; it is no wonder to me that he suffered nightmares for the rest of his life. I share with you now the story he told me that gave him the worst recurring nightmares.

It was July 1942, when Jim was twenty years old and on this particular day the two Japanese guards came for him very early in the morning, kicking him to wake him up. Jim at once rolled in to a ball just like a hedgehog would, for he was now used to how the guards would just pick on anyone to beat up for their own sick amusement, but as Jim looked up he saw it was the two guards that sat behind him each day while he drove the executioner around. They said to him "Speedo bengi. You be quick. Executioner wait for us." Jim thought to himself "who is for it now? Surely it's not me", for he knew only to well that the Japanese carried out many executions at dawn. But he told himself that, anyway, the afterlife must be better than this living nightmare – every day is just one nightmare after another. The guards shouted "Speedo bengi" again at him, and Jim pulled on his old now worn out army boots, and followed the guards off to where the executioner was waiting for them. They all got in the truck and Jim was told to drive on. Jim started up the truck and drove up to the camp gates, where the Japanese guards opened up the gates, bowed to the executioner and waved them through, once out on the open road the executioner shouted to Jim "Speedo bengi", which Jim had learnt by now meant "go flat out as fast as you can!" Jim often thought to himself "I bet if the blooming engine blows up they will blame me for it", but in the six months Jim had with the executioner the old truck never let them down, even though it was badly misused and Jim often had no proper oil to put in the engine. He never forgot this and always said that them Japanese sure can make a good motor engine.

But that was about the only good word he did have to say for them. As he drove along as fast as the truck would go the executioner informed him where he was to head for. After about half an hour they arrived at a small village, made up of old atap huts with their old decaying roofs. Jim thought to himself that they need re-roofing – they looked in a far worse state than what Jim and his mates were sleeping in back at River Valley Camp. The two Jap guards got down from the truck and walked up to one of the huts and kicked open the bamboo door. An old Thai man came to the door-way, and Jim could hear the guards shouting at him. The executioner got down from the truck and walked over to where the old man and the two guards were standing. He spoke to the old man in a quiet voice and the old man ranted back at him, whereupon the executioner just smacked the old man across the face as hard as he could. The little old man fell to the floor. The executioner then stepped back and allowed the two guards to take over kicking the old man; Jim could feel the anger running through his body, yet he knew if he reacted it would cost him his life, and he thought to himself "what can I do to help this poor man?" Jim got down from the truck. The executioner saw this and turned and shouted to Jim in perfect English "you stay in truck." Jim, shaking with rage, did as he was told and got back in the truck feeling totally helpless as he sat and watched this man being beaten. After what seemed like ages the executioner once again stepped forward, and told the two guards to stop. As they did, Jim could see that the boots they had on were covered in blood, and the poor old man just lay there not moving at all. Jim feared he was dead. One of the guards walked over to the truck and took a bucket out of the back, then walked over to a nearby hut that had an old water tank outside it. An old pipe run-ning from the roof of the hut went into the tank, and Jim thought to himself that this must be how they collect their drinking water. The Jap guard dipped the bucket into the tank and filled the bucket with water, he then walked back to the hut where the poor old man lay and threw the bucket of water over him. The old man came to and the executioner instructed the guards to pick the old man up. Jim watched as the executioner then slapped the poor man around the face. Jim thought to himself how cruel the executioner was; as soon as they brought the old man round they tried to knock him out again. This went on for some time and every time the old man passed out, one of the guards would walk over to the water tank and fill the bucket with water and walk back and throw it over the old man.

All the time this was going on the executioner was shouting at the old man – not in Japanese but in what Jim thought to be Malay. After what seemed like hours to Jim, the old man pointed to one of the huts at the end of the village; the guards then just let go of the old man who then just fell to the ground like dead weight. The executioner and the two guards then walked off towards the hut the old man had pointed to. Jim thought to himself how strange it seemed that no one from the village had come out of any of the huts to help the old man, but as far as Jim could see the village was deserted. He could hear the old man groaning as he lay on the ground outside his hut, and so he once again got down from the truck and walked over to the old man. Jim could see that the old man had been beaten so badly that he was near to death. Jim took out his old bit of rag he kept in his shorts pocket that he used to wipe the sweat from his face, he dipped it in the bucket that still had a drop of water in it to moisten it, then he bathed it on the man's lips. The old man opened his eyes and smiled at Jim, then gave a big sigh and his head fell to the side and once again he was motionless, Jim knew that the old man was dead, and Jim being only a young man of twenty, broke down and cried as he held the poor old man's lifeless body in his arms. Jim felt so helpless; he just could not imagine what this poor man had done to deserve to die like this.

As he sat there holding this poor man to him and crying with his emotions running high, one of the Jap guards came up behind him and hit him round the head and shouted at him "you told stay in truck." Jim just looked round at the guard letting the look on his face tell the guard what he thought of him, and then slowly walked back to the truck while the Jap guard went back with the executioner and the other guard to the hut at the end of the village. Jim sat watching them and he noticed that the two guards fixed their bayonets on to their rifles, and that the executioner took out his pistol. All three of them stepped up the three wooden steps in front of the hut on to the veranda. The two guards approached the door of the hut and with their blood stained boots kicked the door open, and started shouting at who was inside the hut to come out. First a little old lady came out of the hut, followed by a young woman holding a small baby; there was much shouting and ranting going on now and the executioner was obviously questioning the two women about something. While the executioner questioned the women the two guards went into the hut, Jim sat in the truck watching, still in a state of temper and shock. He looked at the poor old man who lay on the veranda of the first hut and wondered to himself if the old lady could be his wife and perhaps the girl his daughter.

As he sat thinking these things over in his mind all hell broke out in the hut at the end of the village – gun fire broke out and Jim was startled and quickly brought back to reality. He threw himself down on to the floor of the truck, until the gun fire stopped. The shouting was still going on and Jim popped his head up to have a look at what was going on, and saw that the two guards both had hold of a young man no more then twenty years old. There was so much shouting going on from the little old lady and she was now pulling at the arm of the executioner; she fell to her knees and Jim could see that she was begging the executioner not to kill the young man. Even though Jim could not speak any of the language being used he knew enough to know that the old women was pleading for the young mans life. As she pulled at the executioners arm, pleading with him, the executioner just put his gun that he was holding in his other hand to the old woman's head, pulled the trigger and shot her in the back of the head. She slumped to the floor with blood pouring from her head.

The young woman went hysterical and started to run towards the truck where Jim was sitting watching the atrocious things the Japanese were doing to these poor people. She got to the first hut where the old man lay, shots rang out, and she stopped and fell to the floor on her knees, holding her baby to her breast. Tears were running down her face, and Jim looked at her and with tears running down his face he felt so helpless he could not begin to imagine what these poor people had done to deserve such a fate. The executioner and the two guards, still holding the young man, walked up to the young woman, the executioner prised open the womans arms and took the baby from her. The young woman did not struggle – she just let the baby go. She then bent her head forward. Jim felt sure she was expecting the same treatment that the old woman had received, but the executioner just left her kneeling there. He passed the baby to Jim and walked back to the woman. While Jim sat holding the baby, still shaking with temper and fear, the executioner went and stood by the young woman and spoke to her. She slowly looked up and, her eyes fixed on Jim, she smiled a smile that Jim could never forget; he smiled back at her with tears unashamedly running down his face and as best he could tried to assure her that her baby was alright.

The two guards had now laid the young man down on the ground and had started kicking out at him. After a few moments the executioner shouted at them and they stopped kicking the poor man. As he lay there, the guards walked to the back of the truck and took out some wooden stakes and ropes, walked back to the young man and spread eagled him out. They then drove the two foot long stakes into the ground, one by each stretched-out hand and one by each stretched-out foot, then they tied his hands and feet to the stakes with the ropes. They then stripped his shirt from him, so that he had the full heat of the sun on him (which was in the high hundreds), then drove in two stakes each side of his head, so that he could not move his head. The executioner then told the guards to tie up the woman. They did not spread eagle her out – they just bound her hands and feet behind her and left her where she was kneeling in front of the truck. One of the Jap guards then came back to the truck and took out an old petrol funnel and another bucket, and took them back to where the young man was spread out, then they forced the funnel into the young mans mouth. Jim could see that the young man could not spit it out because he just could not move his head. The two guards then took their buckets

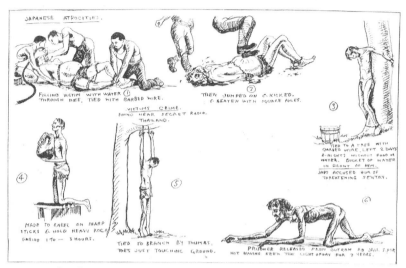

15. Some Japanese pastimes in punishment for minor crimes. The artist experienced similar treatment to the one shown in Fig. 4

and filled them with water from the old tank outside the hut and with the buckets full they came back to the young man and one at a time they poured their bucket of water in to the funnel forced in the young mans mouth. Jim counted about ten buckets full of water went into this poor young man with each bucket holding about a gallon, the young mans stomach was so large he looked like a heavily pregnant woman. Jim could not believe what he was seeing as the two guards then took it in turns to run and jump onto the poor young mans stomach. Jim could not believe the cruelty of these Japanese for as they jumped on the young man's stomach they were laughing to one another – the executioner laughing along with them.

After a while of this sadistic torture, the Japs stopped and poured more water into the young man, and turned the young woman round to watch, but she was in such a state of shock that she just looked down at the ground. The executioner stood behind her and pulled her hair back to force her head up; he shouted at her and Jim felt sure he was telling her to watch the torture being administered to the young man, as the executioner turned to Jim and said in perfect English "you watch you see what happens if you disobey Japanese army". Jim, still in a state of shock and temper, spoke back to the executioner and said what you are doing to these poor people has no honour for you Japanese – you are just a bunch of callous murderous men. The executioner strutted over to Jim and at this moment Jim thought his end had come. The executioner snarled at Jim "you no speak – you just look and learn what happen if you disobey me". Jim swallowed hard and said no more; he sat holding the little baby that he was sure was no more than two months old – it amazed him how the dear little child could sleep through all the noise. He gently cuddled the baby to him, thinking to himself "at least you're safe". He soon looked up again as the guards started to jump on the poor young man's stomach again. After what seemed like ages watching this poor mans suffering the young man's stomach split open, and Jim could actually see the poor young man's stomach spewing out of his body, the Jap guards still laughing to one another at his suffering.

The young woman was still silent and Jim could see that she was just locked in a state of shock showing no emotions at all. Then the executioner shouted out to the two guards, and at once they stepped forward and bayoneted the young man through the heart Jim shuddered with a fear that ran right through his own body; the feeling of pain as the bayonets entered the young mans body.

Jim thought to himself that it must be over now – but how wrong he was. The executioner then ordered the guards to untie the young woman's feet and stand her up. He then began to speak to her, but she did not answer him so he began to slap her about the face. After a while she shouted at the executioner and Jim got the feeling that she was telling him that she knew nothing about what the executioner wanted to know, but the executioner did not stop his questions or his slapping of this young woman's face, but Jim could see that she was not going to answer any questions – she just stared at the executioner and Jim thought to himself how brave she was. After some time the executioner could see that he was getting nowhere with his line of questioning and he just stood quiet for a moment. He then walked over to Jim and once again Jim thought he was coming for him, but the executioner just grabbed hold of the baby and took it away from Jim and walked over to where the woman was standing with the two guards. The executioner handed the baby to the woman, and started speaking to her again the woman spoke back to him now and Jim thought to himself "good, they have finished the killing" and that the young woman must have told the executioner what he wanted to know.

While Jim sat thinking this to himself, he saw the executioner start to smack the woman again; he took the baby back from her and held the poor little mite up in the air with one hand the young woman screamed at him, then the executioner shouted out and at the same time he threw the baby up in the air and the two guards stepped forward with their rifles held above them and as the baby came down they caught it on their bayonets. The young woman collapsed in a heap on the ground. Jim could stand no more and got down from the truck he was shaking with rage and as he got out of the truck he was sick and he fell to his knees and brought up his morning's rice ration. As he looked up he saw the Jap guards just pulling their bayonets out of the poor baby's body. The Jap executioner spoke to one of the guards, and the guard turned round and stuck his bayonet back in to the little babys body and then he just swung his rifle towards the veranda of the hut where the old man's body still lay. The baby's body fell on the veranda like a little rag doll and lay beside that of the old man, both now lifeless. The same guard then walked over to Jim and pulled him to his feet. Jim was six feet tall and this little Jap guard was no more than four feet eight inches. Jim raised his fist up to the guard, but the guard just took a step back and pushed his rifle out at Jims stomach. Jim looked down at the bayonet starting to stick into his stomach and stepped back but he could not move back as he was already up against the side of the truck. He felt sure the guard was going to bayonet him to death, and Jim told me that he was in such a state at what he had seen and how his life was at this time, that he was not worried if the Jap did finish him off. I said to him "how brave of you to be like that", but he said it was not bravery but more like being at the end of your tether when all around you is death and suffering, it would have been a quick way out – perhaps, as he said, even more like coward-ice. But the executioner shouted at the guard, and at once the guard put his rifle down. The executioner shouted to Jim to get back into the truck, which he did.

He now felt so bad he could not cry and just sat with a feeling of numbness running through his body as he watched the executioner move up to the young woman who was still in a heap on the floor. One of the guards came over with a bucket of water and threw it over her to bring her round. As she did so, the two guards held her in a kneeling position and the executioner spoke to her once more. He then he pulled out his large samurai sword, the guards pushed her head forward, and the executioner bought down the sword and severed her head from her body with one blow. Jim had now seen them all murdered and prayed that it was now all over. The executioner shouted to Jim to get down from the truck and help the guards load the bodies on the back of the truck. Jim got down and went straight to the hut where the poor little baby lay; he picked it up in his arms and kissed it on its little head and carried it to the truck he then picked up the headless body of the young woman and carried her to the back of the truck. As he laid her down he placed the baby's body in her arms; he then walked up to the executioner and asked him if he could take the woman's head to bury with her, for he knew that by now his job was to place the heads onto poles as a warning to others not to disobey the Japanese. The executioner bent down and picked the head up holding it by the hair; he looked and smiled at Jim and said "you take head and bury with her body". Jim thanked the executioner for allowing this and took the head and placed it with the woman's body. By now the Jap guards had placed the bodies of the young man, old man, and old woman into the back of the truck. They then all climbed into the truck and instructed Jim to take them back to River Valley Camp, which Jim did, and when back at camp and inside the gates he dropped the Jap executioner and guards off, then made his way to the mass grave that he and other prisoners had dug. He lowered all the bodies into the grave making sure that the baby stayed in the young woman's arms, feeling sure she must have been the baby's mother. He told me how he laid the young man beside them thinking to himself that it could be her husband, and then he lay the old man and woman side by side; he then read a prayer from the old army prayer book that he had kept by him, then he covered the bodies with lime and shovelled a few inches of soil over them. He knew there would be many more bodies to place on top of them before the week was up, although Jim said he could never tell when the week was up because he did this task every day – day in day out – collect the executioner at first light and sometimes not getting back to his hut 'til late at night. His mates used to save him some cold rice, and sometimes he would have a banana to eat with it, given to him by the executioner – Jim could never understand how this man could kill people and torture them all day long, yet he could show kindness to Jim by giving him the odd bit of fruit from time to time, which helped Jim with his vitamins that he knew only to well he was not getting from just two small cups of rice a day that the Japanese allowed him.

Jim told me how he could not erase from his mind the sights he had seen that day; he told me that he saw people beheaded every day, and had come hardened to it, but the sight of the woman smiling up at him and his time spent holding that dear little baby would never leave him, every time he closed his eyes at night the young woman and her baby were there in front of him. As I sat and cuddled him to me in his room at Ely R.A.F. Hospital, we both cried our eyes out. We could not stop and the nurses must have thought that I was as bad as my dad, but this did not bother me for at least I now knew the hell my dear father had been through. We held on to one another and let our emotions cry out. I spent every day for three weeks with my father like this and as you can imagine many of my memories now when I close my eyes at night are of that time spent with him; I now see that I was his psychoanalyst at that time and as I have told you I feel very privileged to have been told these things and I feel sure it was a comfort to my father to be able to tell me the things he did, for, as he told me, he needed to tell some one.

One thing that amazed me was how he forgave the Japanese – a thing his mates could never understand either; many of them have told me of how kind my dad was to them while they were prisoners together on the death railway, and many of them think that is why the Japanese executioner picked him as his driver, because he was so quiet and kind to people. But as my father said, what's the good of being kind to people if you can't help them – just to watch and be helpless is no good to them. But I would like to think that when the young woman looked up at him and smiled at him, it was her way of thanking him for caring for her baby and for smiling back at her to show his kindness when all around her there was hatred and death. This is what I told my dad and I hope it was of comfort to him, even though his nightmares never stopped until the day he died.

The doctors at Ely Hospital sorted out a small war pension for my father, and they told me they were amazed that he had not received a pension as soon as he got home from the Far East in late 1945, not for his mental trauma but for his physical condition, as his left leg had been eaten away down to the bone by tropical ulcers and for the tropical worms still in his blood. I spoke of this to my father and he told me that when he first came home he had gone for many army medicals only to be told "yes, you will be alright in time". Well, I can tell those doctors that he never was; the flesh on his left leg never grew back, and it took another forty five years before the doctors at Ely Hospital cured his tropical worms, yet he never missed a day's work because of it, and he never complained, he just said he was one of the lucky ones for he came home.

And when you think of the two thousand bodies he placed in that mass grave and the fellow prisoners of war he buried in some jungle along the length of the death railway, it's not hard to see just how lucky he had been, and at least I have his grave to visit and put flowers on and a place where I can be alone and talk to him, as he told me all the friends he lost out there in the Far East had no proper grave and their loved ones could not visit and put flowers on their graves like I can. He told me why many of the men won't talk of what happened to them; not because they don't want to, but he told me to remember that when they first came home, most of them were not fit men and some would never be again. As he said, when he visited some of his friends' families whose sons or husbands or boyfriends had not come home, how could you tell them of how their loved ones had died? How could you tell them that the man they knew and loved was starved and worked to death? Or beaten to death by the Japanese to amuse their sick sense of humour? Jim told me if they had been killed in action then you could tell them, for families accepted this, but to tell them that they were beaten or starved to death was a different matter, and this is why many of the men won't talk about what they went through.

The next true story my father shared with me is not so horrific, but sad. It concerns one of Jim's own officers, and to save any shame to his family I shall not mention his name or rank for if he reads this he will know who he is. As I have mentioned, I was going to include this story in my first book but left it out as it seemed some how to spoil the effect I wanted people to have of these brave men, but I have visited so many men while researching this book and most of them mentioned this officer and how he treated them that I could write a book on him, but I shall only share with you the story my father told me of him.

It was while my father was a prisoner on the death railway and held at Chungki Jungle Camp, where he and many of the Cambridge-shire men were being used as slave labour to hack their way through a rock hillside, with just picks and hammers and their bare hands to use as tools, although Jim did tell that towards the end the Japanese engineers did blast some of it with dynamite. Jim was put into one of the rock blasting groups, and he told me how the Japanese engineers would set as short a fuse as they could, and would leave him or one of the other lads to light the fuse, knowing that they only had about five or ten seconds to get clear. Jim told me how he saw many friends killed because they could not get clear in time; he said how once they had lit the fuse they still had to scramble over the broken rock rubble, and most of them had bare feet; he told me how the Japanese engineers would stand far away in a safe position and take bets among themselves as to whether the prisoner would make it to safety or not. If they did not make it, Jim told me, it's not a very nice job having to pick up bits of your friends – it's bad enough when you had to bury their bodies in one piece but when they are all in bits it's even more upsetting – many of the men could just not do it, and it was left to those that could stomach it. Jim told me how being with the executioner had hardened him to the sights of death, he also told me this is another reason men could not talk about things when they got home, to tell a loved one that their loved one had been blown to bits just so the Japanese could have some fun was just not on.

It was during this time, that this young officer who was so scared of the Japanese, started to pick on Jim, Jim had heard the other lads say what a coward this officer had been during the fighting back at the fall of Singapore, but Jim had always given him the benefit of the doubt, but now the Japanese were demanding that British officers must work as well. No work, no food! This scared the young officer so much, and many of the lads now found out where blankets and old rice sacks had gone, they found out that while they had been out working all day this officer had been through their things, and stolen their blankets and any items they had, then he would trade them for money or food from the local Thai traders who camped nearby. This the lads might have accepted if he would have used his ill-gotten gains to help the sick lads, but not him – it was all for his own use, none of the men could trust him as he would just turn them into the Japs, he was in cahoots with most of the guards so that he did not have to work like the rest of the men.

One day when Jim had finished a gruelling eighteen hours work, he and his work party were returning to camp, when this officer stood near the camp gates with one of the guards. After the work party had passed by he shouted out to Jim to stop, and then he called Jim over to him. Poor Jim, who was dead on his feet after such another long day, hobbled over to where the officer was standing with the Jap guard, bowed to the Jap guard, then stood up as straight as he could and said "yes, Sir" to the officer, who then asked Jim for his rank and number which Jim gave him. The officer then said to Jim "why do you not salute a superior officer?" Jim replied "I did not think I had to, Sir, as we are now all prisoners together and after an eighteen hour day, Sir, I just have not got the strength, Sir – all I want to do is lay down and get some rest before tomorrow comes, Sir." The officer said to him "that is no excuse, Bentinck, and as punishment you will now carry buckets up to the top of the hill to fill the water tank." This water was used to cool the drill bits used to make the holes that took the dynamite for blasting, and in the day two men were employed on a two handed water pump to pump water from a nearby river up to the top of this hill to keep the tank full at all times. Jim stood there in total shock – all that he had heard of this man was now being proved to him. The Jap guard soon dug Jim in the ribs with his rifle, and took him over to the river, then with a bucket in each hand Jim had to carry water up to the tank for the next four hours when at last the guard told him he could stop he just fell to the floor in exhaustion. The guard, who had now been joined by two other guards, soon started kicking him; he curled up into a ball as best he could to protect himself, but this did not stop them. Jim could not remember anything then, until he came round only to find himself in one of the death boxes out in the full heat of the sun.

The box was about four feet square, so that he could not stand up or stretch out. He was desperate for water; his tongue felt like leather; he ached all over from the beating he had received, and from the punishment he had done besides his eighteen hour day. He could see it was now daylight but he could not open his eyes as the bright sun was to much for him to bear, he new if he did not get water soon he would not make it, and with what strength he had left he called out for a drink of water from a bucket on the ground out of arms reach of the box. After what seemed like ages, one of the Jap guards came over and took a drink from the bucket he then removed his cap and poured the rest of the bucket of water over him; all of this Jim was watching. The guard then turned the bucket upside down and sat on the bucket and, looking at Jim, grinned to let poor Jim know that he was enjoying watching him suffer. Jim could see two more guards watching what was going on but they stood some way off. After a while, Jim passed out again and only came to when someone threw a bucket of water over him; he could not quite make out who it was who had done him this kindness, as when he opened his eyes the light was to much for him, but he did make out who ever it was had boots and leg gaiters on, and Jim thought it must be one of the Jap guards. He quickly took off his Jap happy, which was all he had to wear, (for those of you who don't know what a Jap happy is, it's something like a baby's nappy, which was made from any old rags that the lads could lay their hands on once their own clothes had worn out) and wrang it out above his dried out mouth, to get what water he could out of it before it evaporated in the heat of the sun, for he was so thirsty, that his lips had already dried and split. He was just so pleased to get some moisture in to his mouth. He then tried to stretch out his limbs as best he could; he told me he sat as best he could and stretched out his legs and arms in front of him and moved them about as best he could, to keep his joints moving. He also knew that he was now very dehydrated; his head was spinning round so fast that he believed he was going to die; he curled him self up into a ball and lay his jap happy over his head to protect it from the sun as best he could, and as he said, prepared his mind to meet his maker, and soon fell into unconsciousness.

He did not come round any more until nightfall, when he came to, shivering with cold for now that the heat of the day had gone it felt so cold. He felt so weak he still thought he was going to die; he did not even have enough strength to call out. He could not see or hear anything and wondered where the Jap guards were. Very soon he heard what he thought to be some one calling his name, but thought to himself that he must be hallucinating, but he kept on hearing his name. He opened his eyes and could see through the side of the box that his mate Percy was there, offering him some water and telling him just to take sips of it, as to drink it down too fast would do more harm than good. He passed Jim some fruit and some rice slop, and told Jim to keep his chin up and not to give in. He told Jim how in time he and the others would pick their moment to sort the so and so officer out and told Jim he would get back to him again if he could. Jim was just so pleased to have some water – he sipped at it best he could and sucked the juice from the fruit, after a while he fell into a sleep again, and remembered no more until the next morning, when the Jap guards came and opened up the box.

Jim told me they looked as surprised as he was that he was still alive. They shouted at him to get out. Jim crawled out on all fours. He dare not open his eyes, for the sun was just to blinding for him. The Japs just left him where he lay. Jim knew that all his mates would be out of camp now working on the railway. He lay there for some time before two other prisoners, who were from the sick hut, came and dragged him to the sick hut where the medics did what they could for him. Jim found out after a couple of days that the two lads who collected him were from the Norfolk regiment, and once he was better he found them and thanked them for helping him. He spent three days in the sick hut until he was fit for work again, but this did not stop the Japs pulling him from his bed each morning and demanding that he worked. When the medics told the Japs that they could see he was not fit enough to even stand, they just hit out at Jims legs with their pickle sticks, until he fell to the ground. After three days of this, even though he still felt so weak and ill, Jim knew he could not go on being hit like this about the legs every morning, so he joined the work party. Without the medics knowing, he went and stood in the fit-for-work line, and marched back to the rock blasting with the others. His mates helped him as much as they could, and Jim was able to sit and break up large rocks with a hammer.

Jim did his best to keep out of the British officer's way from now on, and was only too pleased to leave Chungki Camp to get away from him, for he knew how lucky he was to have survived the dreaded death box, and he knew if the officer picked him out again he might not be so lucky. I think I can honestly say that Jim could never forgive this so called officer, and after the war Jim, like many others, wanted to find him, but his family who were well-to-do business people never had him come home He was sent straight to another country to live, and Jim and the other lads, being only working class lads, could never afford to track him down, so if ever a war criminal got away it was this man, but as I have said Jim did not spend his life being bitter, he got on with his life; he was just pleased to have come home to his family and his sweetheart.

He never forgot the good mates he had lost and every remembrance day he wore his medals with pride, and attended church parades right across the country; places like Norfolk which became his second home, for he never forgot those great Norfolk men who were prisoners in the Far East with him. He bought himself a caravan near Caister in Norfolk, and spent every week end and his holidays there, and visited the friends he had made out there. He also attended Remembrance parades at Leicester, Nuneaton, and Stockingford Church near Arbury Park, where he had done a lot of his war training. I think he did this to feel near to the friends he had lost, as his memories of them here were good ones of days spent training for war together and joking as men do together and enjoying life. My mother tells me that while he was there training she and her friend would go up on the train some weekends to see him and spend the Saturday nights at the local dance; she tells me that there used to be so many of them, but that there was never any trouble – just good clean fun. Even today she keeps in touch with many of the friends she made at that time who still live there, having married local girls and settled there with them and their families after the war. Jim also attended church parades at Northampton, Suffolk, and Hertfordshire to meet up with friends he had made during those dark days, and if he knew that any of them needed help at any time he would be there for them, for that was the comradeship these men had with one another. If only we had it in our society today it would make for a better Great Britain.

When Jim died of a massive heart attack five years ago at the age of sixty nine, I not only lost a very dear father but a best friend as well. At his funeral, the little village church where we live at Histon in Cambridge was packed, with people having to stand in the aisles. The vicar said that he wished it could be like it on a Sunday! There were people there that had worked with my dad when they were only young men and my dad would have been in his forties, who told me what a great influence my dad had been to them when they had been young, for they like me were now in their forties. Other men who were prisoners with my dad shook my hand with tears running down their faces – his mate Percy embraced me and told me how there will never be another Jim for he told me men like him only come along once now and then. Many other men told me how they would not have got through it all without him. Needless to say, I shed some tears that day, and for the months to come, but five years on I think of him with such pride and feel so lucky that he was MY DAD MY HERO.

Footnote

As a youngster, Jim was known to all his family as Jimmy. My grand-mother and grandfather, Jims Mum & Dad, told me as a child, how when they heard Vera Lynn singing The White Cliffs of Dover, on hearing the next line they could not help but cry.

It is
The shepherd will tend his sheep,
the valleys will bloom again,
and Jimmy will go to sleep
in his own little room again.
There will be Bluebirds over
the white cliffs of Dover,
tomorrow just you wait and see,
when the world is free.

Thanks to men like Jim our world was made free, but now these fifty years on I try to imagine what it must have been like for Jim to be in his own little room again, after six years away from it. I know at times it was a thing he thought he would never see again, let alown be able to sleep in it once more, yet it was one of his dreams that had come true. When I was a child and stayed with my grand-parents, I used to sleep in my dads old room which meant so much to me, and now all these years on it means even more to me; and yes when I hear that song I too shed a tear, a tear of happiness, and smashing thoughts of MY DAD MY HERO.

Chapter Two

BILL MOODY'S STORY

Bill as he is today, as over
the years he has lost all of
his old photographs.

Bill was also in the 1st Battalion of the Cambridgeshire regiment
and was in the territorial Army so he was also called up at the start
of the war. He had already had a tough childhood and was brought
up by foster parents, in the Cambridgeshire village of Cottenham.
He told me how he soon struck up a good friendship with my father, and enjoyed his time doing his war training, and told me how
he remembers those happy days spent at Arbury Park near Nuneaton,
and of the good times they all had together at the dances on Saturday nights. He told me with complete modesty of how as a young
man he had a good singing voice, and how he used to get up and
sing with the band on these Saturday get-togethers. I can picture
them now enjoying themselves like young people do, and as I have
said before many of the men came home and married their sweethearts that they met at this time.

One light hearted story Bill remembered was while he and my
father were stationed on the Norfolk coast in 1940 where they were
laying coastal defences in case Hitler invaded. One night they found
themselves sent to guard bombers at R.A.F. Feltwell and Bill told

me how sometimes they were not even real bombers, but just wooden replicas. On one occasion when they were guarding these bombers poor Bill was took short and needed to go to the toilet badly. He said to Jim "I don't think I can hold on mate and I know I can't make it to the toilet," which was at least half a mile away from where they were guarding the bombers. Jim said "don't worry, mate, use the gun pit; just lay one of those old cement bags on the seat and do your business on it, then wrap it up in the bag and we can get rid of it when we finish guard duty," so this is what Bill did, but just as he had finished he heard Jim shout out "Who goes there? Stand and be recognised." He then heard the answer come back – "It's me, soldier. Your Commanding Officer." Jim quickly turned to Bill and said "quick – get your trousers up. The officer's coming." Bill just quickly pulled his trousers up, jumped out of the gun pit and stood to attention. The officer came up to Jim, and he could see that Bill was some ten feet away from where Jim was standing, and the officer called out "good men – that's it. No need to stand together talking. I am pleased to see you two are taking the job seriously. Anyway come with me, I have another job for you two good men." As they marched off Bill said to Jim "what about that lot on the gun pit seat?" to which Jim replied "not much we can do about it now mate. We shall have to get it later." Needless to say, they did not get back there again that night, and the next day they were called before the officer, who told them how one of the gun crew had sat in it. Bill and Jim did their best not to laugh but felt sure the officer knew it was one of them. Bill did try to say "it must have been when you moved us, Sir. Someone must have done it while it was unguarded, Sir." He told me the officer did not answer him – just shouted at them to get out, which they did not need telling twice. As they got out of his office, they looked at one another and just burst out laughing. Bill assured me that if the officer had not come along when he did, the mess would have been buried in the old cement bag, and no one would have even known. Then we both sat and laughed together, which is something that will stay with me in my memories of Bill and my dad for as long as I live, for as you will read, during the research of this book, I shed enough tears with these brave men to last one a lifetime.

After this light hearted story Bill then told me of the day he and the other Cambridgeshires set off for their trip to the Far East, a day they thought might never come, for as he told me, they had spent so long training for war, when they finally got the call they could not believe it, and when they were issued with tropical kit, they thought "how nice", they were going somewhere hot. But, as he told me, little did any of them know the hell that lay in wait for them as they set sail on a very cold foggy morning in October 1941 aboard the SS Orcades. They knew at last they were off to war.

As Bill stood on the deck and saw the coast of England covered in fog, he thought what a great Country he was leaving. He had never much thought of it before, but now it came home to him just what he was leaving behind; his thoughts went back to his time at Norfolk and of his young sweetheart that he had met there; he told me how he had met her at a local dance, and had fell in love with her at first sight; he told me that she lived about ten miles away from where he and the lads were stationed, and how one Saturday night she asked him to come to dinner the next day, as her mum would like to meet him; he told me how the other lads pulled his leg and said that's it Bill you get your feet under the table and you won't go wrong there old mate.

On the Sunday Bill borrowed a bike that one of the chaps had done up, and set off on the ten mile bike ride to find his sweetheart's home. As he came into her village, there she was waiting for him at the village green. As soon as he saw her his heart started to flutter, but before he could say anything she called out to him "come you on – you're late. Mum will have the dinner ready." So they quickly hurried off to her home. Bill said how he felt more nervous at meeting her parents then he ever did when he had to report to an officer. Her mum and dad were waiting for them in their front garden. Bill said how sorry he was that he was a bit late, but the mother replied "that's all right, son. You come in. Dinner's all ready. I'll soon dish it up. You come and sit up the table with father", which he did. It was not long before she came into the room and placed a plate in front of Bill with a large Yorkshire pudding on it and Bill thought to himself, "I've biked all this bloody way expecting a nice Sunday roast and all I get is one bloody Yorkshire pudding." As Bill sat looking at it, the mother said "come on, young Bill. Eat up. Don't let your dinner get cold." With that, Bill ate it up quickly, as he was starving hungry after his long bike ride in the fresh air; but Bill need not have worried for as the mother took away his plate, she soon returned with a nice roast beef and roast potatoes and veg. Bill's face lit up – he poured on some gravy and tucked in. He told me how he was the first one to finish and the mother said to him "you were a hungry, boy. I hope you've left room for some pudding and custard."

But as Bill stood looking at the last sight he would have of England for the next four years, it dawned on him that those lovely days he spent in Norfolk would probably be the best days of his life. He and the other lads were soon given their quarters, and were soon undergoing more training on deck each day. They had a Royal Navy escort for most of the way, and soon arrived in Halifax, Nova Scotia. Like many of the lads, Bill had never been away from England before, and he told me how exciting it was for him, and that after a short stay here they changed ships and Bill went onto the West Point, one of the fastest liners of her day, and set off for Trinidad, South Africa, and then on to Bombay before they arrived at Singapore straight into the action. Bill and his mates soon got dug in and started to take part in the fighting. After three weeks of this, Bill and those dug in with him somewhere in the Bukit Timah area, took a mortar bomb hit and Bill was thrown through the air.

When he came to he was in hospital and in the bed next to him was one of his mates. Bill said to his mate "what am I doing here," and as he said this, he checked himself all over to make sure everything was where it should be. When he found it was, he got out of bed and even though he felt a bit wobbly on his feet he said to his mate "I'm not stopping here, mate. I can't stand hospitals. I'm off." His mate replied "wait for me, then. I'm coming with you." Bill and his mate then left the hospital and returned to his unit. The next day he heard how the Japanese had attacked the hospital, and had bayoneted patients to death as they lay in their beds; Bill told me that he heard that they had done this because some of the Sikhs had fired down on them from the hospital roof, but he could not be sure if this was true or not, but even if it was true it's no excuse to bayonet helpless people to death. Bill and his mate looked at one another on hearing this story and thought to themselves how right they had been to get out when they did. They soon dug in again and got back to the job of fighting the now advancing enemy, but this only lasted a few more days for on 15th February 1942 General Percival signed the surrender at 19.30 hrs. that evening. Bill and his mates could not believe it as only weeks before they had been told that they were expected to fight to the death. Bill told me how he felt pleased that the fighting was over, but at the same time he was worried of what the future now held for them, for he had already seen and heard of the things the Japanese were doing to Chinese and Malays and all of the lads now feared for their lives.

Bill and his company were rounded up and marched off to Changi prison, and was put in to a sand pit, and Bill remembered that the next morning when he awoke how he could not move as he was in so much pain. His mates tried to help him stand up, but poor Bill just could not get straight. One of his own doctors came over to look at him, as they thought he was 'swinging the leg', as Bill put it. But after examining Bill he told him he was suffering from sciatica and rest would be the best thing for it. Bill told me how those around him started laughing, as they knew he would have no chance of rest. Poor Bill struggled on like this for the next sixteen weeks, until it cleared up. Bill was then moved on to River Valley Camp and told me how they were all rounded up early one morning and marched off, those that were sick being helped along by their mates. Bill remembered with a tear in his eye as he told me of the beatings the Jap guards handed out along the way, and how they laughed at the prisoners that could hardly walk, and to make it harder for them, the Jap guards would trip them over, or hit out at them with their pickle sticks. He told me how he received his share of this treatment as he could not stand up straight owing to his sciatica, and he felt sure the Jap guards loved to pick on those who were already suffering. After marching like this for most of the day Bill and his mates arrived at River Valley; he told how he met up with Jim again, and of how they worked together in work parties at the docks, before Jim was taken to drive the executioner. He explained to me how he used to help Jim get over the shock of the things he was having to see and do each day. Bill would save Jim some rice on the nights that Jim was late back, and they would sit and talk together of the things they had seen and done that day.

Bill told Jim he had a present for him one evening as they sat talking, and Jim replied "don't be daft. What present could you get for me out here?" Bill said its something you have needed for some time, and he told Jim to close his eyes and hold his arms out, which Jim did. Bill laid his gift on to Jims arms, and said "alright, you can open your eyes now." As Jim opened his eyes he saw he was holding a large rice sack, he said to Bill "God bless you mate, its just what I wanted." Bill said "I know you did, and I've got meself one as well." He then told Jim how he and Percy had got them while working at the docks that day, and had smuggled them into camp by the guards; Bill said "we must try not to get these stolen like we did our blankets." He told me how they all then used to sit and tell one another stories of life back home, and of how their families must be worrying if they were alright, as they had not heard any word for over a year now. Then one morning Bill said they were all rounded up at first light and told that they were going to a better place, where new camps to Red Cross standards had been built for them with all proper facilities that they needed. Could this be true or was it another lie? When Bill and his mates arrived after a five day train journey cramped into steel cattle trucks, he told me what a poor state they were all in. They were then marched off to a camp called Ban Pong, only to find it to be quagmire – Bill told me they were up to their knees in thick slimy mud, there was raw sewage floating all over the camp from the latrines that had overflowed, and when they arrived at the hut they were to stay in it had no roof on it.

A fellow prisoner already at the camp was knocking together an old wooden box. Bill was shocked to see a fellow prisoner's body being carried out of the hut, by two other prisoners who looked like walking skeletons themselves. Bill and his mates knew now that the Japanese promise of a better camp was just another lie. Even though Bill and the others were so tired and worn out, they knew that they had to try and tidy up the hut and the camp, before they all went down with dysentery etc. They cut the vegetation from the jungle and started to re-roof their hut, and made up brooms from the vegetation as well, with some of the men cleaning out the huts while the others repaired the roofs. Bill told me how the place was alive with bugs and the whole camp was a mass of mosquitos, and as they had no mosquito nets, they knew that malaria would be breaking out soon, Once they had finished work on the huts they started work on digging new latrines in a dryer part of the camp, but found everywhere was just like being on top of a tropical swamp. He told me of the time one of the men sat in the dark one night squatting at the latrines, when he heard someone next to him, the man said "how are you keeping?" and when he received no answer after repeating himself a few times, and feeling sure that there was some one next to him, he stretched out his arm to touch whoever it was. He soon felt an arm and said "who are you?" but when no answer came back he thought perhaps the chap was deaf and can't hear me, so he reached out and touched him once more. He then thought to himself 'this blokes got a very hairy arm', but he soon found out why when a big leathery hand grabbed hold of his hand – he realised it was that of a monkey. The poor chap gave out such a scream and jumped up and tried to run back to his hut so fast that he fell into the latrine. Bill told me the poor bloke was never allowed to forget it until the day he died of cholera about a year later.

Bill found that just as the camp was taking shape, that he was moved on further up jungle to Chungki Camp where he worked the two man water pump that pumped the water from the river to the rock face, the Japanese cook house, and the Japanese wash hut. He told me how one day he was in the Japanese wash hut filling the water tank that fed their home made shower when two of the Jap guards were washing, and when Bill saw one of them lay down a bar of soap it was just to much for him as he had not washed with soap for about two years. As the Jap guards washed with their backs to him he picked up the bar of soap, scuffed the ground with his foot and kicked the bar of soap into the hole he had dug with his foot he then quickly covered earth over it and stood on it with his back to the Jap guards, and carried on filling the water tank. When the Jap reached out for his soap and could not find it, all hell let loose; he flew straight at Bill and ranted in broken English "you take my soap." Bill replied "No, I have no soap. Me prisoner. Me no get soap. You must have used it all up." As Bill said this, his heart was in his mouth, at the thought of what they would do to him. The Jap made him remove his Jap happy and as Bill stood there naked the Jap looked all over him, and when he could find no soap he said no more, and told Bill to go. But Bill returned in the middle of the night and got his soap. He said "it was only a small bar, but it lasted me three months; it felt so good to have this one little luxury and I made it last as long as I could." After a while he was put with the Japanese engineers work party and had to cut the holes in the rock face, by being suspended by rope over the cliff face, with a fifty foot drop below, and how if you did not work fast enough the Japs would tell you that they would cut the rope and let you drop to your death on the rocks below. Bill told me how he saw this happen sometimes and of how on some occasions the victim did not die straight away, but took days to die, with all his bones broken up inside him, and some begging to be put out of their misery. As Bill shed a tear, he told me it's things like this you can't forget or forgive for there is no way to forgive such cruelty – no one alive should treat human beings the way we were treated

After his time at Chungki Bill was moved on further in to the jungle and found himself laying railway sleepers. He found an old petrol can which he and his mates used to boil their water in; they would burn the rice as black as they could then grind it up and add it to hot water to make what they called their cup of coffee. On one occasion, Bill was doing this for him and his mates when the old can fell on him and he was badly scolded over his legs and feet; he crawled along the railway sleepers to try and get help, and as he did this he heard a train coming, so he knew he had to roll down the embankment to get off of the track. This he did but when the train came by him he told me it was only moving at about five miles an hour, and when the Japs saw Bill laying there they stopped the train right near him. Bill thought they had stopped to help him, and as he looked up the train driver released the steam blow down valve, which went straight over Bill's face; he told me how the pain was unbearable, and he was lucky that he had closed his eyes in time, but now he not only had scolded legs and feet but his face as well.

He told me how he must have passed out for he knew nothing more until he came round in the sick hut and he told me how the camp doctor had worked wonders on him to save his good looks. Bill told me how it took months to heal, and he still bears the scars today, which as he says, acts as a constant reminder to him of that terrible day nearly fifty years ago.

Bill was then moved again, force-marched from camp to camp where he lost many more of his mates who were so weak that many of them could not keep up. Bill said you did your best to help carry your mates along, but by this time most of us only weighed in at about seven stone, and we were all so weak it was all you could do to get yourself along let alone any one else. Bill told me how every now and then you would hear a gun shot and would know that some poor chap who could not keep up had been shot through the head, and left where he lay. He said that after a while you got so used to it that you did not look back, you just said to yourself at least he is out of this nightmare, and it gave you that short sharp shock to make yourself keep going. He said "sometimes we were allowed to ride on the trains as we moved up country, and this in itself was a godsend, to be able to just sit and relax even if we were crammed in like sardines. We would sit and share stories of home as we went along and tell one another of what we would do when we got back home, even if at that time many of us thought we would never see dear old England again. Many of us would shed a tear at times like this, even the toughest of blokes would break down at these times."

It was during one of these train trips that they were to see something that confirmed to them all the cruelty of their captors –if it ever needed confirming to them. As they pulled into a siding to allow a train to come by from the other way on the single line track, they were allowed out of the trucks to stretch their legs, and as the other train came by it stopped to take on water which stood in large oil drums at the side of the track. The train was pulling the same sort of old trucks that Bill and his mates were travelling in and the large sliding doors were in the open position as it was so hot and humid. Bill and his fellow captives could hardly believe their eyes at the sights they were seeing, for inside the trucks were badly wounded Japanese soldiers returning from the Burma front lines. There were flies everywhere, and these Japanese men had arms and legs etc missing and none of them had had their wounds dressed. Bill told me you could see blood running from the door of the trucks; the wounded soldiers were begging for water, for Bill had now picked up enough Japanese to know what they were saying, as he had now been a prisoner for three years, he and others said to their Japanese guards "your wounded comrades want water", to which the guards replied "water in drums near track. If they want they get it." Bill said "but they can't walk look they are dying," to which the Jap guards replied "then they are no more use to our great Emperor, they can fight no more so they must die." Bill and the other lads could just not believe how cruel they could be, for these men were their own comrades their own people, not prisoners. As the dying soldiers kept calling for water and help, many of the prisoners could stand it no longer and crossed over to the wounded Japanese soldiers and got them water to drink; Bill said that the guards just looked at them and said nothing, but they did nothing to help. Bill told me how some of them were only young boys and I knew that with Bill only being about twenty-two himself that he meant young boys; he told me he felt sure some of them were no more then sixteen years old. One of them could speak English and he said how sad he was to have to die with out being in his beloved Japan, but he knew his Emperor would be pleased with him. One of the British lads told him just how much his own people cared about him let alone his bloody Emperor – "they won't even give you water when you're about to die, that's how much they care about you lad."

After a while the train had been re-watered and it moved on, Bill and the others stood and looked at one another, and Bill said they were left feeling numb; none of them spoke for some time. They were herded back into the trucks and started off again. Bill said after what must have been an hour one of the chaps said "we bloody helped them – their own bloody people wont help them, yet after how they treat us we are daft enough to help them." No one answered him; they just all looked at him, and he just shut up and sat down quietly with the rest of them.

Bill said after weeks of travelling like this he arrived at what was to be his last prison camp, at Pets Beri. He told how by this time the allied Bombers had been over bombing the railway and how the camp itself had a twenty foot embankment built around the whole of the camp, with Jap machine gun posts at each corner and one each side in the middle, manned by two Jap guards on each. He was told on arrival at this camp, by the Japanese camp commander, that if the mighty Japanese were to lose the war then the machine guns would kill all prisoners. Bill told me how none of the lads disbelieved him, for they knew by now what the Japanese were like. He was put to work on a nearby airfield, and met up with some of the lads he had not seen since the fall of Singapore. He told me how great it was to see them again and exchange stories of how the last three years had been for them all. Bill told me how he once again was put to work on supplying the water from the well to fill the storage tanks that were supplying the water for mixing the concrete etc. He was put with a tall Australian of about six foot three inches, and the two of them would have to pull up the big canvas type bucket from the well and when full it was all the two of them could do to pull it up. All the time they were doing this work, which went on for up to eighteen hours a day, this little Jap guard who they called Gunzo or Gold Rush because of the Gold in his teeth, hit out at them with his pickle stick. Bill said he picked on the Australian more than me I think because the Australian was so tall but me being only small I was the same height as the Jap and I think this went a bit in my favour. One day the Australian took so much from Gunzo that he said to Bill I am going to do for him – I have had all I can take from him. Bill said "don't be daft mate, you know you will only come off worse. Anyway, with all these bombers coming over each night it might not be long before its all over. Keep calm till then and see what happens," to which the Australian replied, "you know what will happen – the bastards will machine gun the lot of us." Bill could not answer this as he believed this too.

One morning when Bill was setting off for work with his work party, he noticed that there was no sign of the Jap guard Gunzo. When he arrived at the well, there was another guard there. Bill knew he dare not mention any thing about Gunzo, but he could not help notice the smile on the face of the Australian. Once the Jap guard was out of earshot, Bill said to the Australian (who's name he could not remember as he always called him Ossie, being an Australian) "do you know where fat Gunzo is?" Bill said how the Australian just grinned at him and nodded his head towards the bottom of the well. Bill said "Oh no, you haven't. We shall all be for it now," but to Bill's amazement he heard no more about it and to this day Bill believes the remains of Gunzo lay at the bottom of that well.

Bill went on to tell me how the Japs never got to use the airfield that he and the others had worked on, as one night the camp was overrun by the Chinese and Malaysian underground army. Bill told me how they pole-vaulted into the camp, and shot every Jap they could find. He said he and his fellow prisoners could hardly believe what was happening, but once it was over they realized how these men had probably saved them from being machine gunned to death, as the Japanese had told them they would be. Bill told me how the Americans then came into the camp and took control, and saw to it that the men got better food and drink –he told me how they all got to eat small meals about six times a day until their stomachs got used to it again; he remembered how the American officer told them of the good job they had done of building the airfield, and that it would now be used to bring in their Dakota planes to fly them all out to Rangoon Hospital where they would all receive the medical treatment they needed. After a few days it was Bill's turn to board one of these Dakotas and he told me how, after all that he had been through, he was never as scared as he felt now, knowing he was going on a plane for the first time in his life; he said there were no seats – you just had to sit on the floor and fasten a rope around you which was secured to some part of the planes structure; there was no door on the rear of the plane and Bill told me he had never felt so cold in his life, he told me to picture them all sitting there with blankets wrapped around them with their teeth chattering, he told me how he can laugh at it now, but then he was just so scared. He told me how the pilots tried to fly as low as they could but even so the altitude was just to much for them as their blood was so thin now that some of the men passed out because their physical condition was just not up to it. He told me how he heard later that some of the planes had crashed into mountain sides because of flying too low, and of how sad it had made him feel to think that these men had managed to survive for the last three and a half years, only to die like this.

He enjoyed his stay at Rangoon and soon started to get on, he heard how the Americans had dropped the H-Bomb on Japan and how this had brought about the Japanese surrender. He met up with more of his old mates and was just so pleased to have come through it all. He told me how he has never been up in a plane since that day, and of how there had been an electrical storm at the time he had made his first and last flight, but he said he just felt safer with both feet on the ground, he had asked the air crew why there was no rear door on the plane, and was told that they had been making food drops to prison camps, so they had removed the door.

Bill was soon well enough to make the trip home, and remembered with a smile what a good trip home it had been. He told me he could not remember all the countries they called at on their way home, but how at every one they did stop at they were treated like royalty, with big brass bands to meet them and thousands of people cheering them. But then, with a tear, Bill told of how when he saw the coast of England again, he and the others could not hold back the tears, for it was a sight they all thought they would never see again, and Bill told me how it had been a thing he had prayed for every night during those three and a half years in captivity. The ship anchored about a mile off Liverpool for it was the middle of the night when they arrived, and the captain informed them they would sail in at 10a.m. the next morning when there were to be many V.I.P.s to meet them, and bands to play them ashore. Bill said that many of the lads were from Liverpool, and that they wanted to jump ship to get home to see their loved ones. That night, Bill said, it was all he and the others could do to stop them from doing it; he told me no one could sleep, and they spent the time talking of their families again; he told me how many of the men had left wives with young babies, when they had sailed off on that foggy day some four years ago; he said how upset and worried the men were that the children would not know them, and Bill told them how he could not wait to get to Norfolk to see his sweetheart again.

The next morning soon came round and the lads got ready. They were glad to have been given army greatcoats to wear, as it felt so cold after the tropical heat that they had been used to. Bill said as they came in to Liverpool it was a sight he would never forget – the noise was so great with people cheering them; he also said he could not forget the sadness of it as well, for many of the men had lost arms and legs, some were blind or deaf etc, and Bill said how when their loved ones saw them, it was the most emotional sight he had ever seen.

At this point I can tell you we were both in tears, and as I gave Bill a cuddle and said "come on, old mate, we can stop now," he looked up at me and said "Michael, I would not have missed it for the world, for in those four years I learnt more about real life than most people do in a whole lifetime." As I smiled at him with tears running down my face I told him how I wished England could have that comradeship today that he and his mates had then, where people pull together and help one another. I then asked Bill what he did when he arrived back in Cambridge, to which he replied, "after a couple of days rest, I went off to Norfolk to find my sweetheart, but when I arrived I was informed that she had gone off with an American. It knocked the stuffing out of me, Michael, I can tell you. He went on to tell me that after that he could never find a girl that he loved as much as her, and that's why he never married, but Bill was not bitter – he had many friends and he picked up his life again and got on.

Bill now spends his retirement years helping his mates who are suffering from tropical illness and mental trauma. For those of his mates that have passed on, he helps to tend their graves, and does all he can to help their widows to get by. He has suffered heart attacks, but being one of the old school he says "I'm alright though, it doesn't hurt as bad as when I lost my sweetheart fifty years ago," but I can tell you she was the one who lost out, for men like our dear Bill are very few and far between.

Bill, thank you for sharing your story with us all – keep up the good work that you and the others do at the Cambridge Yasume Club. God bless and keep you always.

General Tomoyuki Yamashita, commanding Japanese 25th Army that took Singapore.

Chapter Three

ERIC BULLEN'S STORY

Eric was already in the Army Medical Corps when the war with Japan broke out. He had been raised with farming in his blood, and was an expert on farm animals, which was to prove more then helpful to him on more than one occasion in the years to come. He left England on February the 4th, 1940 from Southampton and went across to Calais in France where he boarded a train to Marseille, from where he boarded ship and embarked for Singapore. All the time on this trip, they were training as hard as any of the other soldiers, as there was much to learn about tropical sickness as well as the everyday wounds that soldiers would receive in the fighting to save Singapore. Like many of the other men, Eric enjoyed his trip, visiting many countries on the way; he enjoyed the shopping for gifts to take home for his loved ones, and like many of the men he soon got used to bartering at the local markets for things like gold necklaces, rings etc. These memories were to be the good things to remember of his life at this time

They soon arrived at Singapore, and as they departed ship at Kepal harbour they had time to look around them – not like the lads who were to arrive in two years time, they saw the large guns facing out to sea, and were told how no enemy would be able to penetrate through these defences, so they could all feel safe. Eric was soon put to work in the Alexandra Hospital – and was kept busy. He made lots of new friends, and tells me he got on well with all the nurses, which I suppose is a good thing when you're working with them every day. He was soon put in charge of five or six other medical orderlies and given a hospital ward to be in charge of. He was not one to seek promotion but his commanding officer, Major Davis, informed him that from now on "you are a full corporal and I want to see the stripes on your sleeve," but Eric said how he never did get around to putting them on, for it did not bother him, as he knew the men working under him did as he asked and therefore he felt he did not need any stripes to let them know who was in charge. Eric told me how Major Davis wrote to Fort Canning to let them know that he had been promoted, but still those stripes did not get sewn on, for things were starting to hot up now – the fighting had started and Eric and his lads were kept far too busy sewing up mens wounds without worrying about sewing on two stripes, he said "you can imagine how I felt when in early 1942 all my mates from home arrived with the Cambridgeshire regiment and although it was great to see them again and hear news from home, I would not have ever wished to see them in such circumstances. The lads were straight into action as soon as they landed and towards the end of the fighting many of them had run out of ammunition, but rather than give up many of them fought hand to hand against the Japanese, so you can imagine the sights we were having to see and do our best to save them; sometimes the first time I would set eyes on a mate from home was when they were brought in badly wounded, and all though it was very upsetting, you did your best to save them, knowing deep down there was no chance for them. Towards the end of the fighting the hospitals were so overcrowded, that Major Davis asked me to take over a nearby barracks, so I went off with some of my orderlies and we turned part of the barracks into a mini hospital, but needless to say we too were overcrowded, but two days after we had moved on from Alexandra Hospital the Japanese stormed it and as history now shows they massacred every other patient in every other bed, by bayoneting them to death. They even killed the surgeons and a team who were carrying out an operation at the time – the poor man being operated on knew nothing about it as he was bayoneted to death while under anaesthetic but in this case he would have been the lucky one, Eric said. Just try and imagine the fear those poor doctors and nurses and the patients must have gone through, we knew from then on it was no good thinking just because you wore a medical brasard on your arm, that you would be spared, for there was no excuse for what they did that day at Alexandra Hospital – it was just murder.

It was not long after that our surrender came – a day I will never forget, February 15th 1942, and although I was pleased that the fighting was over, I now feared what would happen to us all. When the Japanese took over we asked for better attention for the badly wounded men; we were told yes they would get it, and they were moved out by truck; we never set eyes on any of them again. We heard shooting down on the beaches for days after our surrender, and we later found out that thousands had been marched into the sea and machine gunned, or they had been taken out to sea by boat and then pushed over the sides. We were soon rounded up and marched off to Changi prison; many of the men were not ready to be moved let alone force marched; we all helped those along that could not make it on their own, these were men who had lost arms and legs, and many of them their sight, and it was these men that the Japanese guards liked to pick on – they would kick their crutches away and then laugh as the poor lad fell down, then they would shout at him to get up on his own; if any of us stepped forward to help you soon got a rifle butt in your back or stomach, or even in the face. Thousands of the men had their nose broken like this, by receiving a rifle butt in the face for trying to help a mate. The boys that were kicked to the ground like this knew if they did not try to get up, they would probably be kicked to death where they lay, yet if they did manage to get up, they knew also that they would be kicked back down again. Many of the lads died from the beatings they received while being moved from camp to camp. I dare say the Japs knew that they would not be able to get as much work out of some one with legs and arms missing, and therefore picked them out for such treatment; it was so heart wrenching to see these lads treated like this and know that if you tried to help you would receive the same treatment, for your life to the Japanese meant nothing; they took great delight in telling us that we were not fit to live because we had surrendered – a thing the Japanese would never do. They told us how it would be an honour to die for their great Emperor but three years later, they were only to pleased to surrender."

On arrival at Changi prison Eric and his orderlies went straight to work with the other medics there and did what they could to help the sick and wounded but as they now had very little medical equipment their job was made so much harder. Eric told me it was at this time he first realised what a good choice he had made in not sewing on his stripes, for he found there were more Chiefs than Indians, and when the time came to be moved on to work on the death railway, they were all told how they were being moved on to better Red Cross-run camps, and that the medical teams could sort out between them who went and who stayed behind in Singapore.

Eric said of course all the officers hearing this promise of Red Cross-run camps thought how good it would be and so told us that *they* would go. "I did not mind at all for I knew by now what liars the Japanese were, and I now know what a miracle it was that I was left behind, for all my friends that went off to find these better camps with all the Red Cross supplies, never found them – all they found was a living hell being forced to build a death railway, and most of them died in one of these disease-ridden camps."

At the same time that Eric's comrades were moving off further into Thailand he found himself being moved to work in the Seletar Hospital and from there he was moved to Kranji naval base camp where he was to stay for the rest of the war. He told me how he had one patient to look after the whole of his three years here, and of what a job he had to keep this man alive; he became very close to this man, and, as I say, he cared for him for three years. Eric told me how this man, whose name was Dick Law, came from Arrington not far from Eric's home, and Eric told me how he had a terrible job to get poor Dick through it, for many a time Dick just wanted to give up, but Eric told him how he owed it to his loved ones back home, to do his best to get home to them, and between them they got Dick through it. Eric told me he followed Dick's life with great interest after that, and he was pleased to see Dick get married and settle down and have a few happy years, even though in the end it cost him his life. Eric remembered with a tear as he spoke to me of Dick, and he told me he was only one of many that had since died young because of what they had suffered at the hands of the Japanese.

While we were discussing these sad events in Eric's life, he told me of his best mate before the war, Mr. Jack Bull who Eric found out had died while being transported to Japan by the Japanese to work in the factories there, but poor Jack like many others did not make it, as the Japanese had loaded so many of these prisoners into the holds of the ships that men were laying on top of one another. The holds were fastened down and there was no air, and as you can imagine the heat was unbearable; if you were lucky the Japs would some times open the doors of the hold and set a hose pipe on you, but this was no good to drink as it would be sea water, but it did cool you down for a while. Eric learnt that while his friend Jack was in one of these holds he suffocated to death, and Eric told me how thousands of men died like this, and how thousands more were just thrown over board once out in the deep ocean, and machine gunned to death and left for the sharks; he told me how all those lovely nurses had been killed, soon after the fall of Singapore; he told me how pleased he and the other lads had been to get most of the nurses onto the last ships to leave Singapore and thought to himself at least if they get to India then they would be able to carry on and help our wounded, but he found out later that the ships

47

had been stopped by the Japanese, and that all the nurses and medical personnel had been executed by firing squad on the beaches, so that they could be of no more help to the British war effort; he told me how he thought them all to be maniacs for, as he said, who else would do such a thing; he pointed out to me how the Japanese would have been better off by using the nurses to care for their own soldiers, but as we have already read, the Japanese did not even care about their own wounded – if they could not serve their little Emperor then they must die.

Eric went on to tell me how many of the Japanese were often the worse for drink, when they carried out torture and killings, rape, etc, and how glad he had been that when the British had surrendered that he had poured every bottle of drink down the nearest drain so that they did not get their hands on it, for as you can see they were maniacs with out drink inside them and with it they were totally insane. Eric was also kept busy at Kranji camp looking after the livestock that the Japanese had, which was mainly pigs and chickens and some ducks. At first the Japanese had looked after the livestock them selves, but found that many of the animals were dying. They checked on the prisoners to find out what they knew about farming animals, and when they found that Eric had a farming background, he was taken to see the Jap officer in charge, and with a Japanese interpreter taken to where the chickens were kept; he was asked to look at them as six of them lay on the ground dead, and found that the Japanese had been feeding them on rice and when the chickens had taken a drink the rice had swollen inside their crop and then exploded as the rice had swelled. They asked Eric what he thought was wrong with them, and Eric told them he would need to see them in the morning light; he asked them what they were feeding the chickens on and one of the Jap guards told him through the interpreter that he fed them on rice. Eric needed to hear no more for he knew what was happening to them now; he was told to come back in the morning so that he could see them at first light as he wanted to. As he turned to leave the hen house the Jap officer said to him "you take these dead chickens and bury them." Eric, not wanting to look too keen said "yes Sir" and bowed to the officer, then he picked up the six chickens and took them and bur-

ied them in a shallow grave as near to the fence of where he and the other prisoners were kept, then in the early hours of the next morning Eric and his mate returned to the fence, and his mate kept a look out for the guards while Eric lay flat on his stomach and pushed his arm under the wire, and retrieved the dead chickens that he had buried the night before.

He then gave three to his mate to carry, and then they made their way back to their hut, he told me how they hid the chickens in case the Japanese checked where he had buried them the night before, but to his amazement they did not. They came for him the next morning and the interpreter asked him if he could say what the trouble was, Eric said that he wanted to see them again and was taken to the hen house. Sure enough there were four more chickens there, and Eric told them how he felt sure that if he could look after them for the Japanese officer, and if they got him some grain to feed them on, that they would be alright. He explained to the officer how the rice had swollen inside their crop and had killed them; he told the officer that this would then poison their insides and kill them. With this Eric thought to himself if they don't believe me I shall be done for, but to his amazement the officer looked at him and said to him "you good man, you now look after chickens and animals for me, you take these dead chickens and bury them, then I get grain for you to give chickens and you look after all my animals from now on." Eric could not believe his luck, he now had ten chickens for the cooking pot and he told me he and the other lads had quite a feast, and from then on every few months a pig would die and the odd chicken, and the grain helped make bread, for as Eric said, man could not live on rice alone, but that chicken and pork sure went down a treat every now and then.

"I feel sure it helped keep many of us alive" he said.

While Eric looked after the animals, besides his other medical duties, he soon got to know which Jap guards to watch out for; he told me that one of the young guards would sometimes come into the sick hut and walk along the ends of the bamboo platforms that the sick men lay on, and one day he dropped a couple of bananas on the beds – he never said a word – just a look at Eric and then he walked out. Eric told me how this was a godsend to the sick lads and they would mash the bananas up and feed it to them, to get a few vitamins into them; he told me how this went on for some time – he would come into the sick hut about every other day, each evening before he went off guard. Then one evening he walked in and walked half way down the hut and stopped at one of the beds. Unbeknown to him, another guard had followed him, and this guard stood in the door way of the hut and was looking down the row of beds to where the young Jap guard was standing, he saw the young guard drop some fruit on to the bed, and then walk on and out of the opposite door at the end of the hut. The other Jap guard looked hard at Eric and the others but said nothing, and just left the hut. It was not long before Eric and his mates and those in the sick hut, could hear the Japanese shouting and ranting on – they felt sure there were no British lads involved as all the shouting was being done in Japanese. After about half an hour of this they heard two shots fired, and Eric told me they never set eyes on the young Japanese guard again,. He told me he felt sure the other Japs had killed him for helping the sick lads in the hut by bringing in fruit. He went on to tell me how that was the only kindness he saw any of the Japanese do for a fellow human.

When the end of the war came and the Japanese surrender had taken place Eric still had plenty to keep him busy – he still had Dick to care for and many others, but he told me they all now had the best medicine needed – better then any medic could give them, for they had now been told they would soon be going home. He told me you could see them start to get better from that moment they heard this news. He said he sat and spoke to Dick about the time they had been allowed to send a card home, during the first year of their imprisonment and of how Dick had said, "it's no good me sending it. I might not even make it through," and Eric had told him "you must send it, Dick. Your loved ones have a right to know that you are alive. Just imagine how they must be feeling not knowing anything at all about us." Eric told me how much it had pleased him when Dick said "Oh alright then. I will fill it in and hope that the Japs send it." As the two of them sat and chatted about that time, they reminded one another that it was two years ago that they had sent those cards off and they sat and wondered if their families had received them, and Eric told Dick, "we don't have to worry about cards or letters any more old mate, we are going to see them again now; we shall be able to hold and embrace one another and put all this damn mess behind us." With that the two men embraced one another and cried tears of joy.

As I sat listening to Eric telling me this story, I tried to imagine what a joy it must have been for them when the Japanese surrendered; it must have been like being given back your life, and being told to make a fresh start. I don't think any of us – how ever many books we read on this subject – will ever know what these men went through or how it felt when they heard the good news that they were free and would be going home. I believe that only those men who were there and suffered at the hands of the Japanese are the ones that know how it really was, but I do know that when they did get home, their families had a very big part to play in getting them well and to help them adjust to every day life again, for I know that many of the men could not adjust and they were unable to hold down their jobs as they had before the war.

Eric and I sat and discussed how the men of the Falklands war had been praised and, as he said, "quite right too", but nowadays the media coverage and television can bring it right to your living room. But in 1942 this did not happen, and therefore people at home just did not know what was happening to their men folk. We spoke of how there was no psychiatric help for the men like there would be today; perhaps that is why so many of the men that are left are suffering from so much mental trauma today even though it's fifty years on; lets hope these brave men can get the help and treatment they need.

Eric went on to tell me of his trip home, still looking after those worse off then him, and of how he managed to get one or two gifts for his loved ones, as those that he had brought on the way out were taken by the Japs. It amazed me that after all these men had been through, they still felt they could not come home with out bringing something from the Far East for their families – many of the men have told me this, perhaps it is something built in us British. I told Eric how the best present their families could have wished for was just to have them home again, and to see them get well again. Eric told me how he went on to be best man for one of his mates that he had known before the war, and who had also suffered at the hands of the Japanese, Mr. Len Miller. Eric said "I was best man for him at Hemsby church in Norfolk, when he married a farmer's daughter, and her sister Lilly was bridesmaid. I got on so well with Lilly that I asked her to marry me and one year later I was back at Hemsby church getting married to Lilly." Eric told me "it's the best thing I ever did" and he and Lilly in time got their own farm in Fulbourn, Cambridgeshire, where they raised their children and where they still live today. Eric and Lilly do their best to help ex-Far Eastern prisoners of war and are members of the Cambridge Yasume Club where Eric is on the committee and with the other committee members he works hard to keep the club running. He told me how there are more widows now as members than there are men that suffered at the hands of the Japanese, but I can tell you those that are left are proud of their club and do their best to keep it going, so they can enjoy that comradeship that they built up over fifty years ago.

God bless them all and long may they enjoy it. I thank you, Eric, from the bottom of my heart for sharing your story with us; God bless and keep you and Lilly safe to enjoy many many more years together down on the farm.

Chapter Four

PHILIP A. DODSWORTH'S STORY

I share with you now another true story from one of my heroes, Philip. A. Dodsworth, who at the age of fifteen joined the Royal Navy with dreams of a great career, and a great future ahead. Once again though, little did he imagine what lay ahead of him.

As a young lad of fifteen, he started his naval training in October 1939, was keen to learn all he could, and after his training, joined HMS Exeter. She had just come out of refit, after being severely damaged in the battle of the River Plate, and Philip and the HMS Exeter were both new and keen to serve their country, the ship having done her part in helping catch the Graf Spee. Philip knew how he and any other new crew members had a lot to live up to, and he was filled with excitement as they steamed out to the Pacific. All of the crew felt sure that if they had to engage in battle then their ship would come out on top, so confidence was very high indeed. They soon engaged the enemy in the Java sea, and after a very brave fight against overwhelming odds, the ship was badly damaged but they did manage to get away, and make for harbour at Sourabaya.

H.M.S. Exeter

It was now February 27th 1942. Philip said they had very little chance of escape as they left Sourabaya at dawn on the 28th of February. "We all knew that the Japanese were shadowing us from the very minute we left port, and not long after enemy ships were sighted, the captain altered course, we lost them and as we were all so very pleased at this we started to congratulate one another on our escape, and then from out of nowhere came a Jap aircraft. He must have radioed our position back to the Japanese ships that we had given the slip, for soon afterwards Japanese ships appeared out of the blue waters, that surrounded us, and we then knew this might be our finest hour when England would expect every man and lad to do his duty – soon the guns roared out, and all of us on board the Exeter knew this was the big one. Our destroyer escorts, H.M.S. Encounter and U.S.S. Pope also knew that it was to be a fight to the bitter end." Philip told me how all he had was a mental view of the action as his station was in the shell room of 'A' turret. He knew all hell had been let loose, from the noise of the shells going off, for the Japanese were now hitting them with all they had, but he told me they never scored a direct hit; but then a stray shell found its way into 'A' Boiler Room. The Exeter had already taken damage to the 'B' Boiler Room from a shell the day before, when she had to escape and make for port, so now with 'A' Boiler Room hit, all power was lost and the screws ceased to turn, although she still seemed to be making some headway through the water.

The crew all carried on their task as best they could, but with in five minutes the thing no sailor wants to ever hear came over the loud speakers – yes – "Abandon Ship" Philip went on to say how his mind seemed to go blank, yet at the same time he automatically made his exit. He made his way from the shell room, up through a hatch, onto a ladder and made his way along the stokers mess deck, up another ladder, and along the marines' mess deck up to the waist of the ship. For those of you like me who do not know what the waist of a ship is, it is, part of the upper deck of a ship which lies

A torpedo being fired from a destroyer.

between quarter deck and forecastle. Philip told me how once here he soon realised what was happening – the ship was sinking, and he now knew he had no choice but to abandon her or die with her. He could see the chaos and despair all around him and (at seventeen years old what ever had he done to be thrown into this) he took a big breath and jumped, noticing as he did so, rows of shoes lined up along side the bulkhead, and he thought to himself "that's us British for you. Always take your shoes off if you are going in water!" As he hit the water, he found it to be nice and warm. He knew that none of the life boats had been able to be lowered away, and knew that he must find something to hold on to so as to keep him afloat; he noticed an oar floating nearby and he struck out for it – it seemed like ages until he got to it as the sea was quite choppy now, and was making it very hard to swim. He knew that anything that was buoyant had been thrown overboard, and as he held on to the oar he hoped that something more buoyant would come along. He could still see his ship but she was listing very heavily to starboard, but she seemed to be going away from him, and after a while she was out of sight, but the noise of battle was still all around him; the vibration of the exploding shells went right through his body; the sky would light up and he would try and look up over the waves to see if he could see any of his fellow crew members; he clung to the oar for dear life, hoping that someone would save him, for he was tiring fast now, and wondered just how long he could hold on; the fear of sharks came to him, and he prayed that all the noise that was going on all around him would scare them away. As he looked up again he could see a carley float coming towards him, and he knew now that if they had room for him, and if they picked him up, he might have a chance of coming through this nightmare alive.

After a while the carley float got to him and already on board was the ship's padré, two officers and at least twenty fellow crew members. Philip said that once he was picked up by them, he felt so much better, not just to be out of the water, but to have company around him again, for as a young lad of seventeen he was still in the grips of an evil nightmare; the other men tried to assure him that they would all be picked up soon, but as they told him this out of the sky came enemy aircraft, homing down on them. They all gasped, and thought they were going to be machine gunned; this fear was with them for some time as the aircraft kept circling above them, but then at last they disappeared, and Philip and his mates were left to bob up and down on the waves wondering what was to be their fate. Philip told me how they spoke of the battle, and those with him told him how HMS Exeter had given her very best, and assured him that the Japs had known that they had been in a very hard sea battle, and that HMS Exeter had done her best to uphold the traditions of the Royal Navy.

It was not long before a Japanese destroyer came in sight, and although some way off, she just sat there; Philip and the others knew now that there was no chance of any British ship saving them, and the fear of being machine gunned in the water came back to him, for he and the others had heard stories of how the Japanese did this instead of taking prisoners. Philip told me that when at sea it is difficult to judge distance, as it can be very deceiving, and although the Jap destroyer looked close to them, it took them a good half hour of hard paddling to get alongside her – rope ladders had been thrown over the side of the Jap destroyer, and Philip and the rest now wondered what was in store for them. With his heart in his mouth, he climbed his way up the rope ladder, to the jeering of little yellow Japanese faces shouting out at him, with no idea what they were on about. He climbed up the rope ladder on to the deck of the destroyer, where he was met by armed sailors and held at bayonet point; as he put his arms up and looked up he could see the flag of the rising sun fluttering in the breeze at the aft of the ship – a great feeling of fear was with him now, for he still thought that the Japs would kill them. Then he was searched, which for him did not take long as all he had on was a pair of shorts. He could see that he and the others with him were the first to reach the ship, and as he looked out to sea he could see that all his fellow crew men were making their way towards the Jap destroyer; he could see that many of them were in a bad way – those that could were doing their best to help the injured, but after about an hour, the destroyer just moved off, leaving many of the survivors still in the water. Philip told me those that survived were picked up the next day – you can imagine the fate of many of them, being in shark-infested waters for so many hours. I'm sure the film jaws had nothing on the things that happened in the water that day and night. It was better for Philip on the destroyer than he thought it would be; the Japs gave him tea and hot milk, and some cigarettes, and blankets for the night; the only thing Philip found was that he could not tell one Jap from another as to him they all looked the same, but he was soon to find out that some of them could be far more cruel than others; he soon found this out when the Japs tried to count them, for, as Philip said, in the whole of his captivity he never met one Japanese guard that could count, and of how after they made several attempts to count them all, the Japs would lose their tempers and start handing out beatings. After spending a very restless night, Philip was glad when morning came, even though he had no idea of what lay ahead for them. They were informed that their destination was to be a small natural harbour on the coast of Borneo, where they arrived before noon, and immediately transferred to a tanker, fearing that they could be off to Japan. They were all now so very hungry, and thirsty, and all they were given were a few ships biscuits and a very small amount of water; when they asked for more, they were soon informed that there was nothing else available for them. One Jap seaman on the tanker asked Philip if he would like some rice, to which he replied, "no thanks, I don't like rice." Little did he know then that rice was to be his main diet for the next three and a half years, and with hunger to overcome he was only too pleased to enjoy what rice he could get.

It was now March 2nd and Philip and the others saw a Dutch Hospital ship which had obviously been captured, being brought into harbour. Later that night Philip and the others were rounded up and the Japanese tried to count them again, but they still could not master it, so tempers frayed again. Once rounded up they were loaded on to invasion barges, and taken over to the Dutch Hospital ship. Philip holding on tight to his blanket, found somewhere to bed down and with hunger pains in his stomach he tried not to think of food; his thoughts as he tried to sleep that night were with his loved ones – he wondered how they were getting on, and that if they had heard of the sinking of H.M.S. Exeter, they would think him to be dead. As soon as he did find sleep he was awoken, and found work to do; later in the day a Jap destroyer came into harbour and came along side the Hospital ship. On board were the rest of the survivors from H.M.S. Exeter. It was now March 3rd so those men had been in the water since 1st March. The men were pleased to see that their Captain was among them, and once all the survivors were on board, food was given to them and the Japs divided them into groups of eight and gave each group a small tin of meat, and some rice, to share amongst them. But this was not enough to kill off their hunger, and still many of them could just not stomach the rice. The next day, things did improve a bit, and they were given a small amount of bread, some dried fruit, and some coffee to wash it down with – also a better system of serving the food was found so as to see that everyone received a fair share.

After another six weeks like this they were informed, that they were embarking for Makasser, which would be home to those that could survive for the next three and a half years. While at sea Philip said how some days they could never quench their thirst as there was never enough water for them, and men would stand queuing for hours and hours to try and get more water to quench that raging thirst. At last they arrived at Makasser, the Hospital ship drawing alongside the jetty at mid day, the sun at its hottest, beating down on the men. Philip had now had his eighteenth which came a week after his capture, but he was still only a young lad and with nothing but his shorts to wear, he was one who soon got sun burnt. He was pushed down the gangplank, as all the men were scrambled off of the ship, to be met by some very vicious-looking Japanese guards, who took great delight in hitting out at them, with their pickle sticks. All the men were craving for water and, needless to say, were all starving hungry, but there was no food or drink for them, for this was no hero's welcome as far as the Japs were concerned – these men were their prisoners. With the help of a Dutch interpreter, the Japs lined all the prisoners up into lines of five men, and once again they tried to count them; the men were left standing like this for hours with the full heat of the sun beating down on them with nothing to cover their heads. Most of them had bare backs and were without shoes, and Philip told me how he wished he had taken a pair from the bulkhead of H.M.S. Exeter before he had jumped overboard. Some of the men had found some old canvas, and they tried to cut bits of this to tie round their feet, for the ground was so hot it was burning their feet so badly, and many of the Jap guards noticing this, would stand on the mens' feet to add to the pain. After a few hours of this, men were dropping like flies to the ground, then at last the order was given to quick march – this order to men that could barely stand, yet being British and with a will of iron to show the Japs they could not be beaten, they marched off, the Captain at the head of the column, leading them off, a total complement of about six hundred, made up of officers and men. Once out on the main roadway the Jap guards soon started handing out their beatings. Men who could not keep up were those picked on; they would be hit with the Japs' rifles, and told to keep up, but once a man fell to the ground that was it, the Japs were on him like flies kicking out at him, with all the hatred they could muster. If any of the other men tried to help a fellow prisoner, they received a rifle butt in their face, and if they to fell to the ground, then they too received a kicking.

Philip told me how he had some of the old canvas tied round his young feet, but it soon worked loose and fell off, but it was more than he dare do to stop and tie it back on, for he could see the cruelty being dished out by the Japs, and knew he just had to do his best and keep going; the men in his line said to him "keep going son, you are doing well. Keep your chin up. Our day will come." Philip told me he was now hopping more than he was marching, as the heat of the road was burning his feet every time they touched its surface. At last they reached their destination, and they later found out that the march they had just undertook was some four miles long, when the shortest route would have been under a mile, but the Jap guards wanted to have fun with them, and so had made them march the longest route. They had arrived at an old Dutch Army barracks, where they were left to stand outside the gates for another few hours while the guards tried to count them again, before handing them over to the prison camp guards.

Philip could see that some men had not made the march, and he wondered to himself what their fate had been, in his heart he hoped they had been spared, but as time went on he never was to see these men again, and soon came to realise what their fate had been. Many more men were starting to fall to the ground now as they stood outside the prison camp gates, and the Japs could see what a helpless situation their prisoners were in. With no fear of retaliation the Jap guards lashed out at them with such viciousness that it still lives on in Philip's mind today and he told me how he received his share of the beatings that day. When at last they were taken into the camp, they were in such a bad way that they knew if the camp guards started on them as well, then many of them would just not survive. Someone must have heard this prayer, for when they at last got into the camp, they were soon divided into groups of forty eight men, and taken to their hut, each of which had been divided into sixteen compartments and five men were put into each even if there was only room for two. The men were now just so exhausted that they fell to the ground hoping that they would be allowed to rest and regain some strength. Philip soon regained his second wind and wanted to explore outside, but the elder men being dubious warned him not to as there was no telling what the Jap guards would do if they saw him wandering about. They asked him to give it time, for they needed to find out what guards they had to watch out for, so Philip sat and rested up for as long as he could, but being young and with that spirit of adventure in him, he wanted to get out and see for himself what the camp was like. Later that night the Jap guards brought them some biscuits, and water to drink, and after having his share of these, Philip could not stand being kept in any longer; he made his way to the door of the hut and looked out, the hut was buzzing with mosquitoes, and flies, and being fed up with being bitten by them, he thought he might as well get some night air, as he looked out he could see in the moonlight that lots of old discarded Dutch clothing, and old blankets etc, lay around the camp. He made his way towards these items, as best he could, dodging the watchful eyes of the Jap sentries, and he managed to retrieve enough clothing and blankets to help him and the others in his hut keep off the mosquitoes. That, in time, would become as big a threat to their lives as the Japs were.

Over the next few days things started to get more organised, the British officers had approached the Japanese in charge of the camp, for better food and medicines for the men, but all they received was rice, and they were told by the Japanese that this was more than enough, but Philip did say that after a few months, they did get some dried fish with it every now and again, but this was not enough to sustain them, so most of the huts set up their own fires to cook whatever extra food they could lay their hands on, as hunger was now the main threat to them. They boiled up grass, but Philip told me he could not stomach this and was sick every time he tried to eat some. One day, though, he smelt a great smelling curry type of smell, coming from his hut when he returned from work. He said to the chap cooking it, "that smells great. Is there some for me?", to which the chap replied "get your tin and you can have some." Philip got his tin and hurried back to get his food. He was dished out a very good size portion, he mixed his rice in with it, and sat back and enjoyed the first good meal he had received since being captured. He told the cook how much he had enjoyed his meal, and how it was the first meat he had eaten since he left H.M.S. Exeter. The cook said "very good. I'm so glad you enjoyed it; all of the chaps in the hut have told me the same." Philip said to him the meat was really nice, was it chicken? The cook replied "no, it was two cats and one dog." Philip said "oh no, I've eaten it" and the cook said "yes, and you have just told me how much you enjoyed it." From then on Philip told me it was very foolish of any dogs or cats, or any animal come to that, to stray into the camp. If they did, their fate was sealed, and the cooks would concoct dishes never heard of before; the stew pots turned out many tasty dishes like this and helped to keep the men alive, and once again I was told man cannot live on rice alone.

Men that were in the work parties went out every day, and Philip told me there were always plenty of volunteers, as it always meant a chance to get more food, and that if any one had any money they could trade with the natives for fruit, sugar, etc. He told me how a black market was set up, and men would bring goods back in to camp, if they could get them past the guards, then they would be sold on a 100% mark up to the Dutch inmates, who at this time seemed to have plenty of money. He told me how men would do anything to get more food, to help them stay alive. Some of the guards could be alright to them at times, and one such guard, when on their party, would hand him his rifle to hold while he went to sleep, telling him first in his broken English, "if sergeant of guard come, you wake me up." They were only too pleased to keep an eye out for him for while he slept as they could take it easy as well, and find some shade from the hot sun beating down on them. Also, while the guard slept, many of the men could slip away and trade with the natives. But as time went on guards like this became very few and far between, and it seemed that only the vicious guards were left, and beatings became all to common.

Under constant threat, of being beaten, men that were not fit turned out for work parties even when they were doubled up with dysentery, and beri beri, for they knew that the Japs would only beat them if they did not get in the line for work, and many of these men knew if they did receive a beating in the sick condition that they were in, then it would kill them, but many men who did turn out for work in this state still received beatings, and many of them met their end this way. Philip went on to tell me how after a while the Japanese moved his Captain and other officers off to Japan, as were the English, American, and Dutch tradesmen who were set to work in Japanese factories as slave labour. This left about a thousand men in the camp, which was made up of the above mentioned nationalities. The Hospital ship that had brought them to Makasser was still in the harbour, and was doing very valuable work in keeping men alive; through consultation with the Japanese it had been made possible for serious cases of illness to be taken on board her, and for a time many lives were saved because of it. The risks those doctors and nurses took to help those poor men – one just can't begin to thank them enough, but as the war went on the Japs took over the ship completely, the doctors and nurses were interned, and soon afterwards the ship left Makasser, and we never saw or heard of it again. As for the doctors, they carried on as best they could in the camp helping to save lives, but the poor nurses were not seen again, but being lovely young women its not hard to imagine their fate.

Life dropped to an all time low now, as food was so scarce, and the men were so very hungry, that it lead to many men taking risks that they would not normally even think about taking – someone was always being caught stealing or trading for food with the natives. This was one thing the Japs were dead against, for they feared we might be receiving information of how the war was going on. Philip told me at that time all they worried about was getting food to keep alive – it never occurred to them to ask if the natives knew how things were going, not until a couple of years later, when they began to realise that the Japs were getting worried, and started to treat them a little better. Philip told me it was six months before the end of the war, when he received his first pair of footwear; then they only issued sandals that were made from old rubber belts. He told me these proved more trouble than enough, as when working in the rain and mud, they were always coming off so Philip, having gone for three years with out shoes, went on till the end with just bare feet, but he told me the only risk with this was that if you cut your foot, or bruised them they soon turned septic, and turned to ulcers, then you were in real trouble, as there was no real medication or bandages – many men went on to lose legs because of them. Philip said one thing that surprised him after the war was how quickly he got used to wearing boots and shoes again. He told me how clothing was so scarce that when a man died, his clothes would be given to those who were worst off for something to wear, but he said some men would be dishonest, and claim clothes, while making out that theirs had worn out, only to be caught trading clothes with the natives the next day, so then to be fair these clothes would be raffled off, but clothes rotted very quickly in this tropical climate, and men never had enough to keep the sun off in the day or to keep warm at night, but then towards the end the Japs issued them with special white shirts and shorts, which they were only allowed to wear on special occasions such as the Emperor's birthday, when they would all have to line up and bow towards Tokyo. As they did this most of the men would then spit on the ground. Philip told me they received much better food on this day, and he and the rest wished that the Japs' Emperor would have more than one birthday.

They were issued at last with mosquito nets, as there had been so many deaths and illness from malaria, which the Japs did not want to catch, but they were made of such very thick cloth with just a small strip of fine net that ran along the top of it, and three men had to sleep under each one. During the rainy season the nights were so very hot and sticky that it was just unbearable to sleep under them, and so many of the men took the risk and slept without one. Philip said he now knows how lucky he and the others had been to be given these nets, for, as he said, those poor lads who were put to work on the Death Railway received nothing; they had to work for eighteen hours a day and sometimes more. He told me "at least we were called by bugle every morning at 6.30am, and we mustered at 6.40am and immediately afterwards we had breakfast, then at 7.30am we had to fall in for work. Some parties walked to work, and some would be taken by lorry; by the time we started work it was 8.30am and work carried on until noon, sometimes if the guards felt kind we had a ten-minute break at 10am. For dinner we were allowed one and a half hours, then we worked on till 5.30pm. But sometimes if a job had to be finished we did have to work right round the clock, without any breaks at all." Some of the work was much harder than other work, and many men would give up supper to a man on an easy work party, to change places with him the next day, and if it was a very hard work party that he wanted to get out of it could even cost him a days food. When the rains set in it made work extremely hard if you were working on aircraft runways – many a time the rains would wash your work away, and the Japs would expect more work from you to make up for it. Philip told me the hardest job he was put on was that of building air raid shelters he remembered having to build one for the Japanese admiral and he had to work day and night until it was finished, these long hours and working around the clock only caused them more illness as it exhausted them so much it just left them weak and vulnerable to sickness. Philip said when you finally did finish work you had a four mile walk or sometimes more to get back to camp, then you would have to stand at the camp gates until the guards felt like searching you, and then dismissed you, then if it was in the hot dry spells all you wanted to do was find water to wash in. There was an old well in the camp, and after swilling down with a bucket of water to remove the dust, and sweat, etc that you were covered in you would at least feel clean; you did not take long though as the well was near to the latrines, and the smell would be nearly unbearable, some times the Japs would allow a bar of soap, which your hut would have to share. Imagine making one small bar of soap last two months between forty eight men – needless to say it did not last. After washing down you changed your work shorts for your best pair and you felt clean and ready for supper, after supper the guards did their rounds inspecting each hut, and by the time they finished it was 9 pm. As the guards entered your hut you would have to stand and bow to them, all orders were given in Japanese, and woe betide anyone who could not understand them – a beating would be sure to come your way. After the guards left most of the men, being worn out, would turn in, ready to face the same thing next day; if we were very lucky we would be given a half day off work every fortnight.

One day while working at the docks towards the end of the war, an allied bombing raid took place on the docks, after which, once the dead had been cleared up, the damage was counted. On one such raid large bales of cloth were damaged, and a lot of it was then given to the prisoners to make themselves clothes with. Philip said what a colourful lot they all looked – more like Joseph and his coat of many colours, but this did not worry them for at least they had something to wear, and one really had to preserve what clothes one had. Morale was higher now as you could sense the allies were now fighting back and the Japs did not like it – you could tell that they were worried. In January 1945, prisoners were dying at the rate of at least four a day; most of the men were feeling very ill and Philip told me it was only that inner sense that things were not going well for the Japanese, that helped keep many of them going. The Dutch Captain in the camp approached the Japs for medicine again, but had very little success.

Philip told me he never realised before just how ghastly death could be, and he told me how he could never describe the sights he saw of men dying, for it is still a thing he has to live with every day – they are all now part of his memory. He told me how he and the others would make coffins out of wood something like orange boxes are made of – "we then put the bodies into them and they were taken to the cemetery on the back of a lorry, and buried. One hundred and sixty Englishmen died in the first few months of 1945, with beri beri and dysentery and malnutrition being the main cause of death. When you returned from work the first question you asked was 'who died today?' A name would be given to you and most times you would reply, 'what a pity. He was a decent bloke,' but after a while you got so used to living with death, that you just hoped that no one died on your half day off, for if they did you had to lose your half day attending their funeral, and when you were so weak yourself that half day meant the difference between life and death to you – it was the only time you really had to rest up and tend to any wounds or injuries that you had. In April the death rate started to decrease slightly, but what would shock you was that you could be talking to a man who you thought looked fit, only to be told an hour later that he had dropped dead; this would come as a real shock to you, and you would start to worry about yourself." Philip told me there is not a day that goes by that he doesn't thank God that he survived.

In August 1945 they all went out working as usual, with no idea of what the day would bring for them. It was 17th of August, and work carried on as usual until about half past eleven when the guards, who had been very quiet all morning, came over and said everyone must go back to camp. The men did not find this unusual and thought to themselves that there must be work at the camp for them to do, but once back at camp, and after they had had dinner, they found out that the main Dutch officer had been with the Jap officers since eleven o'clock that morning, and once dinner was finished all the remaining officers in the camp were sent for. Suspicions were now aroused – something must be happening; maybe a forced march or even mass execution, for we all knew how heartless they could be, such thoughts came so naturally to them. It soon got to 1.30pm and we knew it was not back to work or else we would have been gone by now...... a feeling of such fear came over everyone. Then the bugle sounded muster, and everyone came rushing out of their huts; they were all told to put on their white Jap issue, and return at once, then through the gates marched more Jap guards, which made everyone think 'oh God, they're going to kill us all,' but the guards came and stood right in front of us and laid down their arms. The Dutch Captain came out and went and stood on the rostrum, and then, in Dutch first, followed by English, he announced "THE WAR IS OVER." What he said after that no one heard, and no one cared. Philip said his thoughts went immediately to his home and of all his loved ones, as he stood with tears running down his face – it was a dream come true for him, he remembered back to the time of his first march to the camp, when the older men in his line had told him 'our day will come,' but many of those men had not made it, and with mixed emotions he stood and gave thanks to God. He was now twenty one years old and what a man he had become; he had come through the nightmare. Men spent hours shaking hands with one another, and saying to one another it seems to good to be true, after the excitement died down, they settled back to wait for the occupation force to arrive, they were informed that it would be in a day or two, but they were sadly mislead for it was another six weeks before they arrived.

The Japanese got very scared now and started to bring cigarettes, by the thousands, and better food, toiletries, and an abundance of medical supplies – they even moved them to better quarters. They moved them into a military hospital, and they had even painted in large letters outside – "PEACE CAMP" but as Philip said, it was to late for them to repent now, the lives they had taken and the beatings they had given, they now deserved all they got. Philip said how everything changed now with more and more cigarettes coming in each day, there was fruit, bottles of beer, even whiskey and brandy, but he said ninety per cent of it was meths – also the allied planes had now spotted them, and were now dropping supplies, to them as well; he told me they traded the cigarettes that the Japs gave them, with the natives, for such things as ducks' eggs, chickens, ducks, and sugar and cake, etc, and because of all this when the allies did finally arrive, most of them had put on about a stone. On the day the allies did arrive there was only a small force of them at first and there was much activity from the Japs preparing for their arrival – they were doing all they could to make it look as if the prisoners had been living a life of luxury, but the state of most of the men would prove them wrong, but it amused all the lads to see the Japs actually working.

When the allied ships were in sight every one soon got to know and made their own way down to the docks which was about two miles away, it was such a wonderful sight to scc thc allied ships at last, it really brought home to everyone that we were really free at

Destroyers at sea.

last, all the Jap big wigs were there, waiting and any Jap not so important was busy serving us all with drinks; a large marquee had been put up and we all sat under it in the shade, having our glasses filled, which the Japs were only to eager to do for us – oh, how things had changed. These same Japs were telling us, only a few weeks before, that there was no medication, or food and drink, available, other than rice, now they were falling over themselves to give us the stuff; they even thought that the Australians that had arrived to take over were going to sit and have tea with the Jap officers – they were soon disillusioned, as the Australian officers in charge soon let them know that they were certainly not here to have tea with them.

It had taken the ships over two hours to get into the harbour, as the entrance was still strewn with mines, and the Australians were taking no chances. Once in harbour, Jap coolies tried to tie up the ships, but to make a proper job of it Philip told me he and the other lads did it themselves, and then within an hour of arriving all the ships' bakers were cleaned out of bread completely, and Philip said 'oh, how good that bread tasted – our first taste of bread in over three and a half years.' It truly was a moment to savour, for back in the Hospital rice was still the main food, but no one was eating it, as most of the men were getting their meals on one of the ships now in the harbour. After a few days the men heard that a ship was waiting for them just out side the harbour. Philip told me how they were all taken out to the ship by a small Australian frigate for, owing to mines, it was still very dangerous for ships to get in and out of the harbour, and once again the men thought to themselves 'don't let us hit one of them now –*please*', for all they wanted was to get home safe to their loved ones now that the war was over, but although they were now free, they all still had a great fear that something awful could still happen to them – could there still be a Jap submarine out there that did not know the war was really over? Would they hit some unexploded mines? All these thoughts went through the mens' minds. Philip told how three men did die some weeks after the war, from the tropical illness they had contracted. It was so very sad to see this happen – to go three and a half years, with such hardships, and come through it all to die a few weeks after was a real downer for all the men. As Philip told me, it really was the survival of the fittest. As they got out of the harbour and out to sea, Philip stood looking back at the coast line of Makasser, growing fainter, until at last all that was visible was the outline of the mountains; it suddenly came home to Philip that he really was going home, he really was free – and he stood and cried tears of joy, and gave thanks to all who had helped him through such an awful nightmare. The frigate arrived at the ship waiting for them, which turned out to be a Submarine depot ship, and great was their delight when they heard they were bound for Western Australia, and five days later they arrived at Perth Harbour. By a strange coincidence, it was Sunday, and it seemed strange to Philip that it should be on a Sunday that they were sunk, and a Sunday that they came back to civilisation.

It was the first Sunday that Perth harbour had been open to the public since the war, and thousands of people had turned out to meet them. As they drew alongside, they were greeted by a band playing and streamers flying, and Philip said it was such a nice sight to see all those friendly white faces cheering them in; he also told me that to set eyes on a white woman again was also something to savour. Once the ship had tied up, the sick men were taken off first, and taken off to Hollywood Hospital by ambulance, then the fit men were called upon to disembark, but Philip stressed to me when he says fit men, of whom he was one, they would not be classed as fit today by any means – men who weighed in at around six stone, but were able to walk, were classed as fit men, even though they were suffering from tropical illness, ulcers etc; if you could walk, you were in the fit party.

Philip was taken to a large warehouse, where he and the other men were kitted out with new clothes etc, then a large tea had been laid on for them by the ladies of Perth. Philip can still remember today the sight and taste of all those lovely cakes he had that day. After tea they went on to H.M.A.S. Leeuwin, the Royal Navy barracks, where at eight o'clock supper was served to them by the Wrens, then everyone was so tired that they all went to bed, or as Philip puts it in his nautical terms they all "turned in". "The next day was spent having medical investigations, lots of X-rays etc, lots of pills and injections, and then after a day or two of treatment, those that were passed fit were allowed leave. A very Grand lady named Phylis Dean, an Australian, made it possible for all of us to really enjoy it, for she arranged for us to visit the country, or stay in the city, whichever we wanted to do." Philip went on to say that he chose to visit the country, and travelled some two hundred miles to the south of Perth, to a place called Bussleton, where he stayed for, as he put it, eight glorious days. He told me the Australian people showed him such hospitality that it was beyond all praise, and this was something he heard from all servicemen that he came into contact with in the years to come, and even today Philip still speaks just as highly of the Australian people.

After his glorious holiday he was taken back to Perth, and as he was waiting to board the bus, he saw a man nearby digging a trench, and after his three and a half years of using a shovel, he said to the man "would you like me to lend you a hand while I wait for my transport?" to which the man replied "what service are you in then cobber?" "I am in the Royal Navy" Philip replied with pride. "Oh no, you won't be any good – you Sailors don't even know what a shovel *is*, let alone use one!" Philip said he could have made a rude remark, but didn't – he just smiled back at the man and said "oh alright, good day."

His bus soon arrived to take him back to Perth, and once back, he had a couple of days to look round before they left. It was a weekday when they departed from Perth, but still there were lots of people to cheer them off, and once out at sea they all felt quite sad to be leaving those kind Australian people, but the happiness in their hearts of soon seeing their loved ones again helped them through it. Most of the men were feeling so much better now, and the eighteen days it took them to reach their next port of call went very slowly, and they found the time started to drag. This told many of them that they must be really getting better, for it was not so long ago that if anyone had offered them the chance to just sit back and relax on an eighteen day cruise, it would have been a dream come true – but now they were feeling better, they just wanted to get home. They arrived at Capetown, where they stayed for eight days, and once again the crowds were out to greet them; during this eight day stay Philip and the others spent time getting presents for their loved ones back home, then after the sightseeing it was goodbye Capetown, and off to Gibraltar, where they stayed for just two days. The excitement was getting to all of them now, knowing that it would not be long before they could see and hold their loved ones once again after nearly five years; some of the men got so excited that it made them ill, for even though they thought they were now fit and well they were far from it really – many of them still only weighed in at eight stone, when five years before they had weighed in at around thirteen stone, or more. The medical staff advised them not to get too excited and they would be alright, but how can you tell men not to get excited after five years of hell, and knowing that you were only a couple of days away from seeing the loved ones that at times you thought you would never see or hold again.

They soon departed from Gibraltar, and soon arrived at Portsmouth, to be greeted by thick fog, which delayed them getting in, and also delayed them from seeing the sight they had dreamed of for the last five years – yes, those beautiful sights of the England they all loved so much. After waiting offshore for some hours, the fog started to clear in the afternoon, and at last the men could see their beloved homeland once more – they stood and cried tears of joy, and spoke to one another of their families; some of them had left wives with small babies, some had brothers and sisters in the services and were all hoping that they had got through it all OK. As they stood and chatted like this, before they knew it they were in to port, and tied up alongside H.M.S. Wolfe. There were hundreds of relatives waiting in the crowds to meet those men of H.M.S. Exeter. The Mayor of Exeter greeted them all with a message over the loudspeakers, and then they were allowed to leave the ship, and get down that gangplank, and stand once again on dear old Blighty. Philip told me "it felt oh so good". All that was left for him to do now, was to get through the routine back at barracks, of sorting out ration cards, cigarettes, Red Cross presents, and then get off to catch the first possible train out of Portsmouth.

It was early evening before Philip got away on the 12th of December. He travelled through the night, back to his home in Southwell, Notts, and arrived at Nottingham station at 3am. He found a taxi and set off for that home he had dreamed of for the last five years. When he arrived it was all in darkness of course, but once those inside knew who it was, it was not dark or quiet for long. I shall leave you to imagine the scenes that went on in that house that morning and for the days that followed, when Philip had time to look around him and to reflect on all the suffering he had been through. To one day get back home had been his dream, and, as he told me, he was one of the lucky ones – he had come through, and for him it was "HOME SWEET HOME".

All that remains for me to say is a big thank you to you Philip for sharing your story of those terrible days in the forties, and to wish you good health, long life and happiness, to you and your family – God bless you all.

Chapter Five

BERT GRIMES' STORY

Bert was born and raised in Norfolk, in the village of East Rudham near Kings Lynn, where he grew up with the great British countryside all around him, and often played at soldiers with his mates. Little did any of them know at that time that they would grow up to become real fighting soldiers. As they played at soldiers in the local woods, they would imagine they were fighting in some tropical jungle – on a hot summer's day it was not hard to imagine that they were in the tropics, but in time they were to find out what real tropical heat was like.

Bert's time soon came to leave school and set out into that big wide world, but he still never imagined that within three years he would be on his way half way round the world. He got him self a job as a young cable layer, as it was at the time that local villages were starting to have electricity laid on for them; the days of the old oil lamp were on the way out. Young Bert worked long and hard at his job. He told me "in those days, you dug the trenches and laid the cables – no machines to dig for you." He was very happy at his job, and can still remember the day he came home from work, when he was a young eighteen year old, to be told by his parents that a very official looking letter had arrived for him. As Bert undid the letter and read it his heart came up in his mouth – yes, it was his call-up papers. He was so happy at his job and this was the last thing he wanted at that time. He was asked to report the next day to the Kings Lynn Drill Hall and sign up. Bert went straight off to see his boss and told him about his call-up papers, and of why he would not be at work any more. His boss told him not to worry – the war would soon be over, and he could come back to work with them, but little did any of them know that it would be some six years later before that day would come round.

After signing up, Bert was sent to Norwich and put with the 5th Norfolks. He kept his head down and did as he was told, and it was not long before his Sergeant Major told him he was to be put forward for the Regimental Police of the 5th Norfolks. Bert told me he thinks it was because he was tall and looked the part, but he soon gained respect of the men, and they were not to much trouble to him. After some months of training, they were sent off to Liverpool to help with the blitz. Bert enjoyed his time here as the Liverpool people are so kind and friendly they made the lads soon feel at home, but orders soon came through that they would be joining the 18th Division and were off to the Middle East. Although there was excitement at the thought of going abroad, there was also the fear of the unknown – what was to be their fate; they were told not to worry and just enjoy the voyage of a lifetime. Bert sent off his last minute letters to his family telling them how much he loved them, and not to worry as he would soon be back, but this was to be the last they heard of Bert for the next four years, not knowing if he was alive or dead. I ask you to just imagine to yourself what it must be like, to just have a loved one taken from you, and not to know anything of them for the next four years; only those really involved in this nightmare will be the ones to know what it was really like.

The morning soon arrived when they were to embark – tropical kit had been issued and the men were already for the off. It was a foggy day when Bert boarded the Duchess of Athol and thought to himself how this was to be home for the next few weeks, and as they departed, Bert and his mates stood and took one last look at dear old England and Bert told me how they all hoped it would not be long before they would see her again – many of the men were not ashamed to shed a tear, as many of them were only young lads of eighteen or nineteen, and this was the first real time that they had to take in what they were leaving behind.

Bert and I spoke of all the things one takes for granted in life, and he told me that, as they steamed out of Liverpool that day, he stood and thought to himself of how precious, those everyday things in life were, for he now knew he was off to war, to fight for his country, and for all those precious things he had always taken for granted until now. As he stood with his comrades watching those last sights of England slip out of sight, he knew that there was no turning back now – like thousands of the other lads, the boy now had to become a man. As they settled in and tried to find their sea legs, many of the lads spent most of the time being sick, and the thought of food just made them feel worse. Men would joke to those feeling sick that what they needed down them was a good plate of fried eggs and bacon, then they would laugh to themselves as the poor chap they had told this to would start to reach, and rush to be sick again – but no one really minded as it was all part of the mens' banter between themselves, and once they did settle down to life at sea there was still plenty of training to do and things to discuss. They had a royal navy escort, but the fear of being torpedoed by a German submarine was in most of the mens' minds, and they were not sorry when they arrived at Halifax, Nova Scotia, and were able to feel their feet on firm ground again.

After a few days shore leave, they boarded another ship, this time the American liner Mount Vernon, which was to take Bert and his mates half way around the world, calling at such places as South Africa, Trinidad, India, and many other ports of call. Bert and his mates enjoyed the sights in the few days they had in each port, and they all realised how well they had lived back home, as there were beggars everywhere, and Bert could see that life was very hard for these poor people. Meanwhile back on board ship Bert and his mates were living like Kings with so much good food being dished up by the American chefs, which made Bert feel quite sorry for the poor hungry people begging at the docks and in the towns, and

Bert and his mates would take food to them to share with their families, for at this time none of them knew what real hunger was, and as young men far from home it upset many of them to see so many people going hungry. Little did they imagine that before long they also would know what real hunger was.

They soon set off again still not knowing where their final destination was to be, but after a few days out they were informed that they were off to Singapore, to fight the Japanese to stop them from taking Singapore. No time was lost. The ships went at full speed ahead while Bert and the others were issued with maps of the area, and told to study them. The men spoke to one another about Singapore, with many of them saying "we should be OK there. It's one of the best defended islands that we have." They told one another of how they had heard of the large naval guns that had been set up, and of how nothing would get in once they opened up, but little did any of them know that the Japanese had come across through virgin jungle that the British intelligence service had believed no one would ever be able to get through, but as history now shows to the fate of thousands, the British intelligence were oh so wrong. After a few days they arrived, and, as Bert told me, they arrived in an almighty thunderstorm; most of the men had never seen rain fall like it did that day, but they gave thanks that at least it kept the Japanese air attacks off while they landed. As they departed ship and came down the gangplank, most of the lads feared being washed away, as it was raining so hard, and when they were told that they would be making camp that night at Kepal harbour, the lads thought to themselves 'how can we put tents up in this weather,' so most of the men camped for the night in the open. Some of the chaps put boards across old oil drums to make shelters to get under, to keep the rain off as best they could, but into the evening the rain eased off, and the Japanese air force attacked the docks in force, this was the first taste of action for the men of the 5th Norfolks and the gun crews were kept busy that night, and for the next few days and nights. It was on one of these nights that poor Bert was badly burnt. During one of these air attacks, Bert was close to oil drums ignited by the Japanese air raids, and as well as being caught by the flying shrapnel, he suffered very bad burns. His chums around him who

77

had not been hit, did what they could to smother the flames on him, but by the time they could get to him, Bert had been badly burnt – he was semi-conscious, and the medics knew he had to be taken to hospital as soon as possible. For Bert the fighting was now over, but the struggle for life was just beginning.

He was taken to Johore hospital, where the doctors and nurses worked miracles on him and pulled him through. Bert found himself with many of the men from the navy ships' crews, who like him had been badly burnt in action when their ships had been hit, and they had been forced to abandon ship, with many of them having to jump into burning oil floating on the sea. As Bert told me this the memories all came flooding back to him and he broke down and cried, and as I sat and cried with him I said "let's leave it now, Bert. It's so emotional for you," but Bert, as brave as ever, replied "no, I want people to know what I and my comrades went through for their today."

After a time Bert was well enough to travel, and he was moved by truck, and informed he was being taken to the docks to board a Red Cross ship that was about to leave Singapore for Australia. The truck was driven by an Indian driver and another young Indian went along to help them, but as they arrived near the docks an air raid came, and Bert could hear gunfire all around him. As Bert and the others lay in the back of the truck, all they could do was hope that they did not get hit, as none of them were well enough to make a run for it – bullets went through the canvas roof of the truck, but luckily did not hit any of them, and after a while the attack was over. It was some time before they heard British voices speaking nearby, and so they all called out, and soon found a head of some one coming in the back of the truck saying "what are you lot doing here?" Bert and the others told him how they were to board the Red Cross ship to leave for Australia, only to be told that the ship had been badly damaged in the air raid and would not be going anywhere for some considerable time as much work now needed to be done before she could sail again. As Bert and the others cursed their luck, one of them asked where the Indian driver and his assistant were, only to be told that they were no where to be seen. Bert never did know if they got killed in the attack or whether they just ran off as he never saw them again. Bert and the others were taken to some government buildings that were now being used as a make-shift hospital, and the medical people told them that as soon as the ship was repaired and ready to go they would be on it, but that day never came for Bert, as a few days later the Japanese took Singapore. Bert told me how he lay on his bed when the Japanese soldiers came rushing in, a chap in a bed near Bert had an old wind-up gramophone, and the first Bert saw of the Japs was when one of them stopped the music by putting his bayonet through the gramophone. As Bert heard the music come to a sudden stop he opened his eyes and looked up, to find little yellow men looking at him and shouting at him, while pointing their bayonets at him; he could not understand what they were shouting at him but did his best to get up and put his hands up. With no consideration for his wounds, Bert was pushed and shoved outside, with all the rest of the patients – what the fate of the doctors and nurses was Bert did not know, as he never saw them again, but as he looked at me I knew only to well what their fate had been. Bert and the others were made to stand outside in the full heat of the day, and left like this for many hours, with many just collapsing on the ground, and left where they lay – many of them were not at all well, suffering from severe burns and bullet wounds. No water was given out and the fear of what was going to happen to them as they stood and looked as the Japs set up machine gun posts around them, was just to much for many of them to take, with many of them saying "why don't they just get it over with. If they are going to shoot us why don't they get on and do it, not just let us suffer like this?"

After hours of just standing in the full heat of the day, there were more men lying on the ground than there were standing up, and the Japs took great delight in putting the boot in to those on the ground to add to their suffering. As evening fell, a little Japanese officer arrived and after speaking to his men, Bert and the others were pushed and shoved into rows of four across, by about fifty men long, making up a total of some two hundred men. They were then force-marched to Changi prison. As Bert marched off, he looked around at those poor souls left laying on the ground – he knew that many of them would be dead by now, and thought to himself how for them the nightmare was now over, but he was soon brought back to reality as a Jap soldier dug him in the back with his rifle butt and shouted at Bert to keep up. Bert told me they looked a sorry lot, with most of them being badly burnt it was all they could do to stand up let alone try to march, but they all helped one another along, and by some miracle they all made it to Changi, where they found the worst problem to be the mass overcrowding. There were no toilets or washing facilities and just one standpipe to serve over 17,000 people with water. Needless to say, men spent all day queuing to get water, to quench their endless thirst, for men like Bert who were still suffering from burns or wounds, this meant relying on a friend to get some for you.

After a while the medics got Bert round, and the day came when he had to line up for work, it was about 6am and he lined up with the others to be counted, a thing the Japanese could never do with out inflicting a beating on to someone. Bert and his comrades soon learnt to count in Japanese, for if they did not shout out their number in Japanese, they soon received a beating – Bert told me how he lost many of his mates like this over the next few years, and, as he said, if you stepped forward to help a mate who was being beaten, you received a rifle butt full in the face by one of the other guards. As we spoke of this Bert asked me to try and imagine having to stand and watch your best friend beaten to death, knowing that if you tried to help you would end up the same; he told me how at first your natural instinct was to move forward to help your friend, but after you were beaten a few times you soon realized that if you wanted to stay alive, you just had to stand and watch, for at the tender age of twenty life is so very precious, and to stay alive, and the thought of home, and your loved ones was what kept you going. After being left to stand for about another hour, they would then be marched off out of camp. The work party that Bert was in went down to the docks, and he had not gone far when he noticed a row of heads laying on a table top – about six in all, they looked like Malays and Chinese, and their headless bodies lay in a heap under the table. Bert could still remember how the Japanese guards laughed as they looked at the heads on the table, and he soon learnt that they had no regard for human life other than their own.

Bert and his work party had about a five mile walk to the docks, and once they arrived they were put to work unloading ships, which they did until nightfall when they were marched back to camp. On the way back to camp Bert saw another six Chinese bodies that had been bound in barbed wire; they had then been shot through the back of the head and had fallen into a ditch were they had just been left. Once back in camp Bert was issued with his few ounces of rice and his mug of muddy water called stew, after which he found some- where to lay his tired body to rest for the night, ready to face the same thing the next day. This went on like this for the next couple of months, before Bert found himself being marched off to Farrow Park Camp, where he met up with the Gurkhas – the men from Nepal who were renowned for being excellent infantrymen, and fighting soldiers, who were hated by the Japanese, and Bert saw many of these brave men beaten to death. I remembered my own father telling me that a Gurkha never drew his knife or bayonet with out drawing blood and dear Bert confirmed this for me.

Bert was now put to work in and around the old Ford Motor Company factory – and the work was very hard, consisting of cut- ting down large trees and loading them on the back of a lorry, then to save petrol the Japanese guards would make the prisoners pull the lorries along – ropes were attached to the front of the truck, then with five men on each side they would be made to pull the truck along. If they came to a hill it was often all they could do to get it to the top, then as it went down the other side, they had to pray that the Jap driver would hold the lorry back on the brake. As Bert told me this he broke down again, and I can only imagine that he had some bad memories of this, for as you can imagine if the Jap did not hold the lorry back on the brake, and if those poor men close to the front of the lorry could not get out of the way in time, you do not need me to explain their fate to you. After six months of this hard work on very poor food, Bert was having his share of ill- ness. Many of his comrades had been shipped off to Japan to work in the mines and factories, but Bert was informed he was being sent off to a Red Cross camp that had just been built further up in Thai- land. He was informed that once there he would receive proper care and attention, and proper medication to make him well again, and so Bert and his chums were marched off to the railway, where they boarded the metal cattle trucks that I have mentioned before. These were to be home for the next five or six days and nights, and for Bert and those who were now quite ill, it was to be no picnic. To this day Bert still has nothing but praise for his comrades who helped him through those dark days, for without their care and help he would not have made it. After a few days of travelling they passed by Ban Pong camp and saw fellow prisoners, and Thais, and Chinese, and Malays, working on the railway. They soon realized that they were not off to any Red Cross camp, and now knew that all they could look forward to was more hard work and starvation. When they arrived at Wampo, there was no camp for them as it had not been built yet, so they just slept in the open at the side of the river, and they were put to work on cutting down the teak trees which, as you may know, is a very hard durable wood just right for building bridges and viaducts. Wampo is now famous for its Viaduct – it cost many lives to build, and is a place Bert and his comrades will never forget.

Bert was now becoming very ill through dyscntcry, malaria, and jaundice, and the work was just to much for him, but he knew 'no work – no food', and he did his best to keep going. He told me how he enjoyed working with the elephants that would pull the trees along and told me how he found them more intelligent than the guards, but the day came when he just could not keep up and so he was moved on to Takanun. Bert was very lucky indeed to reach Takanun alive for he was now so very ill he knows that he only stayed alive at that time because his chums cared for him so well; the Japanese guards took great delight in picking on the sick for they knew that they would get no work out of them, and when one of the guards went to pick on Bert, his mates knew it would be the end for Bert in his condition, and so they intervened between Bert and the guard and took the beating instead. I don't think it even entered the guard's minds what they were doing, and I imagine as long as the guard vented his hatred on one of them he was not bothered – it's no wonder to me that men like Bert and all those that suffered at the hands of the Japanese, have such a wonderful comradeship.

Once at Takanun Bert soon found himself in the sick hut with severe dysentery, malaria, and jaundice – he was also tested and found to be a carrier of the cholera germ, the thing the Japanese guards feared most, so Bert soon found himself being moved again, this time to Tamarkan sick camp back down the line. Poor Bert could hardly stand let alone walk, and when he was lined up with the others to leave camp he told me how he looked a very sorry sight indeed as they were marched off to head for the river, where they were to be transported by barge. Many of the men could just not keep up and Bert was one of them; as he fell to the ground, he did his best to get up but as he tried to get to his feet, he was kicked back down again by one of the guards, and received a severe kicking. He did his best to roll up into a ball, but did not really have the strength even to do that. As he lay there receiving this kicking, he thought this to be his end but the thought of ending up just left to rot away on the edge of the jungle was not for Bert, and he mustered all his strength and got up, whereupon the Jap guard shouted at him "you keep up or you dead." Bert did not need to be told this for all around him there were men dropping to the ground, and for those who could not make that great effort to keep going, they received a gunshot to the head, or a bayonet through the heart, and were just left where they lay.

At last they arrived at the river and were put on to the barges. It was heaven just to be able to sit down at last and rest; the men spoke to one another of those who had not made the trip, and said how at least their suffering was over, but by the time they reached Tamarkan many of them had also died. Once they arrived Bert was put into Tamarkan sick camp where he was so ill that he needed a blood transfusion. A young Borneo boy of about fifteen years old gave Bert four pints of his blood; the young lad had seen all his family killed by the Japanese, and he told Bert he was only too pleased to do what he could to help Bert keep alive. As Bert lay on an old table with the young boy on another table beside him, the medical chaps tried to find a vein in Bert's arm, and placed an old bit of small rubber tube into it, then the same was done to the young boy; then as the young boy lay pumping his fist to pump the blood into Bert, he told Bert how he would help look after him until he was well again, a thing Bert has never forgotten, and Bert to this day will not have any one in his presence say any thing unkind about coloured people, for Bert knows this lad's kindness saved his life.

Bert started to get on after this blood transfusion and received a bit better food while in the sick camp, and he soon felt that bit stronger and the day soon came when the Japs wanted him for work again. He was sent to Chungkai to work, and after a month here he was sent on to an area near Kinsioa. He travelled by rail this time, and was soon put to work on bridge building but he was not strong enough for this type of work, as none of them were, but they knew to survive they must do their best to keep going and they would help one another the best they could. It was one such day as this when Bert and his pal Bill, were trying to fix in a large teak log support to a span of the bridge that they just did not have the strength to hold and they dropped it. It fell some 40ft below and by some chance managed to fall on top of a Jap guard. Needless to say, he met his just deserts that day and Bert and his mate thought they would be thrown off of the bridge, but to their amazement a Jap engineer nearby to them told what he had seen and said how it was an accident, but the other guards made Bert and Bill stand to face the sun, standing to attention. After some hours of this, they started to sway and then the Japs shouted at them to keep still, but because of the heat of the sun and the amount of time they had been made to stand like this, they just could not keep still, so in moved the guards and beat them with their bamboo pickle sticks until they collapsed, and then the Jap guards had some other prisoners drag Bert and Bill back to camp, where their mates dressed their wounds and cared for them.

A few days later Bert was sent for by the Jap officer and told that he would be going back down the railway with another prisoner to meet some high ranking Japanese officers who were coming to visit the camps, and to inspect the work being done on the railway. Bert was told he must do as they say and carry their belongings for them; the other prisoner to accompany Bert turned out to be a mate of his from the Royal Corps of Signals, and he and Bert could not believe their luck – they enjoyed the trip back to meet the high

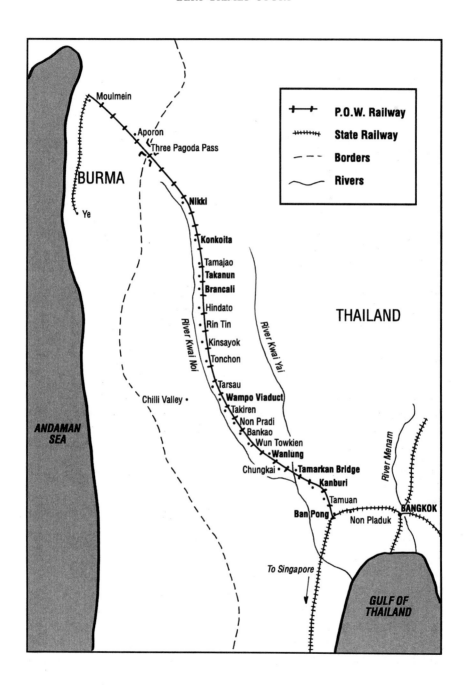

ranking Jap officers as the rest from hard work done them the world of good. Bert told me how he had to polish the officers' knee-high boots, and act as valet to them. Bert and his pal travelled the entire length of the railway with these Jap officers, and they made sure they had some of their food, making sure that the poor lads in the camps got some of it as well, whenever they had the chance to get it to them.

Bert and his pal saw for themselves the suffering of all the men in these camps, also of the forced native labour force, where he saw men women and children worked to death. He told me nothing mattered to the Japanese; all that was on their minds was to get the railway finished and it did not matter to them how many prisoners or natives died, as long as it got finished. Many a young Thai girl was taken from the work parties to entertain these high-ranking officers, some only about twelve or thirteen years old, but to stay alive they knew what they had to do. Once the officers had inspected all the camps, Bert found himself sent back to Chungkai camp, where he was given the job of killing buffalos for the Japs; he told me of how you had to put ropes around their necks, and then with two men each side pulling on the ropes to try and strangle the buffalo. He would have to hit them with a sledge hammer between the eyes to try and knock them down, and he said that many a time he would be worn out before the buffalo, but once the buffalo did drop to the ground, you had to cut its throat and catch the blood. Bert and his chums made sure that buckets of this blood got to the sick camp, where it would be cooked up like liver for the sick lads. Bert told me how he had his share of this and the tripe from the buffalos stomach – after just eating rice and the odd snake, this was just so good, he told me.

The allied bombing raids were starting to come now and Tamarkan bridge was badly hit, and many of the British prisoners there died in these raids. As Bert was now one of the fitter men he found himself being marched off to Tamarkan to work on the bridge, and he was put in a work party that was piledriving to repair the bridge – this is the bridge many of us call the Bridge over the River Kwai. The Japs would also make them dig out any unexploded bombs, and many of Bert's mates met their end doing this job – the

Jap Guards made sure they were well out of the way when this was being done, but they let the lads know that they would have them in their rifle sights, but as Bert said, there was nowhere to escape to and the men were in such poor condition that it was all they could do to get by each day, without the added fear of what would happen to you if you did try to escape. Bert and I spoke of one of my heroes at this time, Mr. John Sharp of the Leicestershire Regiment, who tried to escape soon after being sent to work on the death railway. He was captured, and for the next three years and two months, he was held in the torture gaol in Singapore, twelve months of which he spent in solitary confinement – he was one of the worst treated of all the prisoners of war, yet he survived – yes, a hero indeed.

One day while working on the bridge the Jap officer asked for a small work party of five men to leave the camp and live in the jungle, cutting down trees. Bert volunteered and was given the job of driving an old truck to bring the trees back to the bridge; Bert told me how they carried fifty gallon petrol drums on the truck with them, about four in all, and whenever there was an air raid the Jap guards would make the five of them sit on these petrol drums. Dear Bert had bad memories of this for he had already been badly burnt as you know, that night at the docks some three years earlier, and when the Japs made him sit on these drums he feared being burnt once again. Then one night he was driving the truck to Kachanburi and as he stopped to have rice for the Japs at his camp loaded onto the truck, a young Thai boy came to the door of his truck and said to him "very soon you go home, then he ran off." Before long he came walking by again and came as close to the truck as he could, and he looked at Bert and said "Churchill number 1 now." When Bert arrived back to camp he told his mates of what the boy had said, but the others told him "Bert, get to sleep. You have been having nightmares", for they were already asleep and did not like it much because Bert had woken them to tell them his news. But the next morning as they arose they could sense something was not right, for instead of work they were loaded into the truck and Bert was told to drive back to Chungkai camp. When they arrived they found that nobody knew what was happening. On the way to

Chungkai they had seen some Thais waving Union Jack flags, and yet still the thought that the war could be over never entered their minds.

Once back in Chungkai, all was quiet and the Jap guards seemed very subdued. No work parties were called for, and the men were left to just relax and chat amongst themselves, and all types of rumours were being put around the camp, but as they all turned in for the night, Bert told me how in his heart he hoped and prayed that this nightmare was coming to an end at last. The next morning they were awoken by the sound of the drone of aeroplane engines, and as they came out of their huts to find somewhere to shelter – expecting it to be an allied air raid – they found that they were Dakotas dropping large bundles and leaflets. The leaflets were quickly picked up by the men, and when they read that the Japanese had surrendered an almighty cheer went up around the camp; the fitter men collected up the bundles and found them to have medical supplies in them and tins of fruit etc, which were taken to the medical boys. For those too sick to know what was going on, friends explained to them that it was now all over and that they would soon be free to go home, but as I have mentioned before, some of these poor men were in such bad condition, and got so excited that they had massive heart attacks and dropped dead; the medical boys had quite a job on their hands to keep the men calm, but as Bert said to me, just try and imagine the emotions on that day. He told me how it was like being saved from hell, for yes, these men had been in hell on earth for the last three and a half years – the fittest men in the camp weighed about six stone and most of the others were under five stone and could only crawl round on all fours.

It was not long before the Japanese officer in charge of the camp sent for the Dutch and British officers to talk of the surrender, the leaflets had stated that the Japanese should be left in charge of the camp until the allies arrived to liberate them, but many of the men did not agree with this, and wanted their revenge on those guards who had beaten their friends to death, and had caused them all so much suffering. But when the officers returned from their meeting with the Japanese officers, they informed the men that no reprisals were to be taken, and that these Jap guards would receive their just rewards in due course, but a few of these guards were never to be seen again. Bert left it to me to think what their fate might have been, but when you think of how deep the latrines were in the camp, I'm sure they received a few of them.

After a few days the allies arrived and Bert and his chums were taken by truck and rail to the nearest airfield where they were flown to Rangoon hospital, where, like most of the men, Bert met Lord Mountbatten, a man they all had great respect for. Bert told me how through just a short chat with him, it made him feel so much better – to know someone like Lord Mountbatten appreciated what you had been through for your country meant a lot.

Bert soon started to put on weight, and soon found himself on the ship and on his way home. At last the freedom he had dreamed of for so long had come to him; he and his comrades were all over-come with emotion as they first saw the coast of England again – a sight many of them had thought they would never see again, and they all stood and had a quiet moment with their thoughts of those last four years in their lives, and of those thousands of men who they had left buried back in that vast jungle. Yes, they knew they were the lucky ones, but they knew they would never forget their pals who had not made it back, and as they stood looking at dear old England Bert remembered how, some four years earlier, he thought it would not be long before he saw England again. Never did he imagine that it would be four years later, but here he was again and he and his mates gave thanks to God that they had come home at last.

Bert and the others were cheered as they came ashore, and they were just so pleased to see their own people once again. They were then taken to transit camps for further tests for the next couple of days, before being allowed to leave for home. Once Bert received his train pass and read the words Kings Lynn, he knew he was on his way to his loved ones at last, and as you will know by now it is just too emotional for me to write about, so once again I leave you to imagine those scenes as Bert arrived home at Kings Lynn station, and saw his family again; what a great moment for him and his family, for they were to be the ones who had to care for him now, for Bert, like thousands of others, had been told 'there is your freedom – now get on with life', but after all he had been through it's not quite as easy as that, and that is why today when these men that survived this nightmare see how the soldiers of todays wars receive psychiatric help it angers them to think how they were just told to 'get on with life.' Dear Bert has suffered with his nerves ever since coming home, and later on in the book I shall explain why many of the men have had this problem with their nerves.

As Bert settled back in to life at home again, his friends and his family were the ones who helped him to get on, and in time he did start to get on; he told me how he had many jobs until he felt settled again – he went on to meet his wife Rotha, and together they had five children, and today they have twenty grandchildren and two great grandchildren. Bert went back to the far east in 1984 with some friends and he laid a wreath on behalf of his Regiment in remembrance of all those who did not come through; he visited the camp where the young Borneo boy had given him his blood, and prayed to himself that the young boy had survived and was also enjoying life somewhere; he went back to the Kwai and slept out in the open near to the river, just has he had done all those years ago, and he gave thanks that he had been able to come back and see it all under better conditions. As he stood there in thought he only wished that his wife had gone with him, but she had been to afraid to fly, but Bert's dream did come true, for the very next year he and his wife returned together – she overcame her fear of flying, for as she told me, all her Bert had been through she knew that she had to be there with him to see for herself the places where her Bert had suffered so much, and they now have some happy memories of the place to share together. They loaned me the video that they had taken on the trip, and my wife and I found it of great interest, to just see how wonderful they looked together with their comrades enjoying themselves. Bert and Rotha are now planning to go back for the 50th anniversary, and all I hope is that they remain fit and well to make this trip together, and to enjoy many more happy years together with their family. God bless you Bert for what you gave for our today.

Bert back at Kwai.

This is the nearest Bert could find to the petrol drums they were made to sit on during air raids.

91

Chapter Six

ROBERT DRIVER'S STORY

I share with you now another true story from another of my heroes, Mr. Robert Driver, a man who has suffered so much, yet with the help and love of his dear wife Doris he has come through it all, and he shares his story with us now.

Robert was born in Norfolk in the village of Grimston, and on that day he had a brother born as well, for you see Robert is a twin. He, like Bert, grew up with all that lovely open countryside around him, he may have even been one of those young lads playing at soldiers, in the woods with Bert. Oh, what wonderful times. But as us older ones know, those childhood days go far too quickly, and Robert soon found it was time to leave school and set out into that big wide world. He found himself a job as a young trainee gardener, working for Colonel Handcock at Congham Hall. Robert enjoyed his work, and as a young lad of 14 he found he was soon given his share of the hard work, but he got on well and Colonel Handcock soon saw what an asset he was to his work force. Over the next four years Robert worked hard for the Colonel and learnt all he could about the land, and when in 1938 all the rumours of war in Europe started to circulate, Colonel Handcock asked Robert if he was happy working for him, to which Robert replied "yes, Sir. I am very happy at my job." Colonel Handcock said, "you won't want to be going off to war then, will you lad?" Robert replied "no, I don't really want to go to war, Sir." Colonel Handcock told him to go along to Kings Lynn Drill Hall and join the Territorial Army. He told him how war might never come, but at the same time he told Robert that if he was a member of the Territorials it would be much better for him – something Robert still can't understand to this day.

Robert went home that evening and talked it over with his parents and they advised him to see what his friends thought about it, so after discussing it with them, he went off to see his friends and they all agreed it would be great fun to be part-time soldiers, and go to camps etc. Little did any of them realise then that as soon as war came, they would be the first to be called upon to fight for their country. The next night they went off to Kings Lynn to the Drill Hall, and joined up with the Territorials. This was early in 1939, and Robert and his friends enjoyed the next few months – they enjoyed their training, attending church parades, and going away to camp, but these happy times went far too quickly, and when Hitler started to invade the rest of Europe, Robert and his friends soon found that they were summoned to report to Dersingham Drill Hall, where they signed up to be full time soldiers.

Robert found himself in the 7th Norfolks and found himself billeted for the next few months all over Norfolk. He worked at the docks in Kings Lynn, and along much of the coast line, putting up invasion defences to keep the Germans out. It was now late 1939 and word came that the 7th Norfolks were to be moved off to Aldershot ready to be mobilised to the action, but as Robert was only eighteen at this time he found himself left behind, and put into the 5th Norfolks, but at least many of his friends stayed with him, and Robert soon found he knew some of the lads in the 5th anyway. The next year was spent doing lots of training and Robert and his friends found themselves fitter than they had ever been, and felt ready to take on anyone; they would sit and talk together about how they would soon sort those Germans out once they got at them, but they had no idea then of the type of men they would end up having to fight against. Robert's regiment was now moved off to Scotland to finish their war training. It seemed that things were moving fast now and Robert soon found himself leaving Castle Douglas in Scotland to board the Duchess of Athol with orders that they were off to fight in the Middle East, after calling at Liverpool to pick up the rest of the 5th Norfolks, they set off and Robert, like the others I have mentioned, stood with mixed emotions as he saw the coast of England slip out of sight. He stood alone with his quiet thoughts of home and of what his family would be doing at that time, and of what his workmates of Congham hall would be doing. As he stood there thinking of home he soon realised that he was a world away from all those he held so dear to him, and he stood and made a silent prayer that it would not be long until he was back with them all again.

Robert and his mates soon reached Nova Scotia Canada, where they transferred to the American liner the Mount Vernon; there were two other American liners that sailed with them, with one brigade on each. They were now informed that they were off to fight in the Middle East, and after being issued with tropical kit the men had no doubts that this was true. They soon arrived at Trinidad and took on more supplies before moving onto Cape Town, South Africa, where they were allowed to spend three days shore leave. Most of the men enjoyed this and to this day those that survive have fond memories of their few days there; for Robert and his mates it went far to quickly, and they soon found themselves sailing off again. They were told that they were now off to India, to Bombay, but within three days of reaching India they received orders to turn around and head for Mombasa. When they arrived at Mombasa, Robert and his mates were given another three days shore leave, and Robert and the others wondered if they were going to war, or were just to enjoy cruising the oceans of the world, and while on shore leave they joked amongst themselves of where they would cruise to next for a few days break, we now know that they were being used as political pawns while the powers that be made up their minds whether to throw them into Singapore or not. Once back out at sea the orders were confirmed and Robert and the others were informed that they were off to defend Singapore.

The liner steamed off at full speed ahead now to get to Singapore as fast as they could; last minute lectures were given to the men, and Robert remembered with a smile, how his officers had told them all, not to worry as the Japanese could not see more then ten feet in front of them, as their eyesight was so bad owing to their slit-type eye sockets. Robert can laugh at this now, but at the time he told me that he and the others quite believed it, but as he was to find out oh how wrong those officers had been. Robert had now been at sea for nearly three months; on his ship were 6,700 men plus 600 crew, and they arrived at Singapore on 13th January 1942 – as I told Robert, unlucky for some. As they embarked from the ship, the men were in the worst storm they had ever seen, with the rain washing down the docks and streets like rivers, but at least it kept the Japanese air force at bay which saved a lot of the men at that time. Robert told me how unfit they all were, after being at sea for just over eleven weeks, with no room to exercise, or train, and it felt good to be moving about at last, although he was pleased to be loaded into trucks to be moved off to a transit camp, where they stayed for just two days. While here the news was broken to them that the Japanese were now already on parts of the island, as instead of coming by sea they had come across through the jungle. Robert told me that it was from then on that he found that everything he had been told about the Japanese was so wrong. He and the others had been told that the Japanese were so afraid of the jungle, and that they had no idea of how to live off the land, but now they were being told of how the Japanese had come for miles through virgin jungle to take Singapore. Robert told how when you are young and naive you don't stop to question your betters – you just believe them, but from this day on Robert told me how he started to trust his own instinct and perhaps that's why he is here today.

He and his mates were soon on the move, and they found themselves being sent to Hihitam where they dug in at the side of the roads, it was here that Robert saw a complete section of his unit wiped out, which included many of his own friends. As they crossed through a ravine, the Japs had set up a hidden machine gun post, and as the men walked through the ravine, they were just massacred; they just did not know what hit them. Robert and the others then had the job of taking out this machine gun post before they could move on. Many more lives were lost that day until it was taken; Japanese snipers were all over the place, and Robert soon found that there was nothing wrong with their eyesights, for many of Robert's mates got picked off like flies with out even knowing where the shot had come from. After taking this position and digging in, Robert found himself being moved further into Johore to Batu Pahat. Here Robert got dug in again, and took some of the worst fighting; he knew that the 6th Norfolks were dug in further behind him and the 2nd Cambs were further back at Sangarang, but the Japanese had now managed to get behind them, and had dug in and set up road blocks, so that Robert and his mates could not go forwards or backwards. After days of heavy fighting, ammunition soon began to run out, and all that was left was to fight hand to hand, with your bayonet; Robert lost many of his best mates at this time and he told me how even to this day, the sight of those friends dying at your side still comes back to you.

At last his Commanding Officer gave the order to retreat. He told them not to worry, as by the time they got back to Sangarang the Japs would have used up all their ammunition, and the Cambridgeshires would have them licked; Robert told me oh, how he and his mates prayed that this would be true, but when they arrived at Sangarang they came to a big bridge, and all the wounded lay along the side of the road. Robert had never seen such sights, or so many wounded men before; men were crying out in pain for someone to help them, even begging to be shot because they were in such pain. As Robert crossed the bridge there was Padré Duckworth standing there; he

Fighting in Johore.

96

shook every man's hand and told them it was now every man for himself; he told them to choose between making for the sea or the jungle, and wished them all the best, and said God bless and keep you safe. Many of the men will remember Padré Duckworth for his bravery and help to them in the death railway camps – a hero indeed, God rest his soul.

Robert and his chums chose the jungle, and set off with thoughts running through their heads of what they could do to stay alive; as they got deeper into the jungle they decided to sleep by day and travel by night, for fear of snipers was still the main threat of death; they lived off coconuts and they drank the milk from them. After three days and nights of this they found themselves back behind British lines, and were so pleased to see friendly faces again.

They were now back in Singapore, and found that all the civilians had been moved out. Robert told me how in most of the houses the tables were just left with food on them, and he and his mates lived like lords for a few days on the tins of fruit and meat that had been left behind in these houses when the occupants had fled Singapore. Robert was now mixed in with the Cambridgeshires and even men from other Regiments as things were really getting bad now, and men that had retreated found themselves with men from other Regiments, but this did not bother them as they knew only too well that they were now all in the same boat, so to speak. Robert found himself held up in a Chinese cemetery, and he and those with him joked to one another how if they don't make it out of the graveyard at least they won't have far to go to be buried, but as Robert told me, this was just mens' nerves talking, but for many of them later that day their talk of this was to come true. The officer in charge informed them that it was now the 14th of February and he urged them to hold out and not be forced back; in the fierce battle that followed this officer lost his life, and with no other officers left Sergeant Len Gilbey took command and led his men on into battle. Len took the men of his platoon and told them and Robert that the colonel had told him that they must fight to the last man, so there must be no pulling back. Robert and the others thought this would be the final hour and when Len gave the order to attack they were with him. A Jap machine gun took many of them out, and sergeant

Len Gilbey's arm was shot to pieces, but with the arm just hanging on by a few threads of skin he fought on until they had taken and held their position, it was then and only then that he passed out; some of the others then carried him on their rifles to the medical station where his arm was amputated. Sergeant Len Gilbey went on to receive the Distinguished Conduct Medal, the highest award to anyone in the Cambridgeshire regiment serving in the Far East.

For Robert and the others, on the very next day, February 15th, came orders that they were to lay down their arms at 4pm as they were to surrender; they were told to dump any ammunition that they had left, and Robert and his mates were in a state of shock, for they had prepared themselves to fight to the death. Robert told me how they dumped all their remaining ammunition into a dyke, then he and his mates sat and talked to one another of how their mates had died over the last few days, and how that, now they were to surrender, in a strange way he and the others felt cheated, for they had prepared themselves to die for the cause, and as Robert told me, they quite expected to be joining their friends that had already died. At 4pm that day, 15th February 1942, the order came to lay down their arms and surrender, as this was the time General Percival had agreed with the Japanese when he had signed the surrender, but we now know that 4pm to the Japanese came two hours later owing to the time difference between our two nations. When our boys laid down their arms at 4pm needless to say, the Japanese went on firing for another two hours, during which hundreds more of our boys met their end. Robert and those left with him spent that night catching up on sleep, for they had not been able to sleep at all for the last week.

In the early hours of the 16th of February the Japanese Imperial Guards came and took Robert and the other prisoners. "They were not too bad to us," Robert said, "they wanted to know if we had any food, and soon took all our cigarettes for themselves, and any food was taken as well." They told them not to worry as they would treat them well, but they did say how they could not be sure how the other Japanese and occupation troops would treat them. Robert spent the next two days with these Imperial soldiers, and he told me that in that time they were kind to him and the others.

Soon trucks arrived and they were taken to Changi prison where, on arrival, they were put into the old NAAFI building and left to fend for themselves. Robert told me how they were some of the first to arrive at Changi, and the sights he was to see over the next two weeks as hundreds of thousands of fellow prisoners arrived, soon made him and his mates realise just how lucky they had been to have been brought there by truck, as many of the men now arriving had been force-marched there, and thousands of them were near to death from the beatings they had received along the way. Robert and the others did all they could for these poor souls but sometimes it was just too late. At first there were no proper burial parties, and so bodies were just piled up in a corner of the camp – I'm sure you can imagine the smell, and the flies that this bought, and as there was no food issued in the first week to ten days, things were very bad indeed. For Robert in the NAAFI part of the barracks at least he had somewhere to lay, but for thousands of the men there was nowhere to rest, as the Japanese had crowded so many prisoners in, that many of them could just not find any room to lay down, for fear of being crushed to death. As I have mentioned before there was only one stand pipe with a slow running tap, to serve over 100,000 men with water. Needless to say disease soon broke out, and caused a very big headache for the medical boys, but soon the Japanese started to make work parties of many of the prisoners, and Robert was put into one of these, and found himself working at the docks, and clearing up the bomb damage in the streets of Havlock Road. He remembered having to load up hand carts with all the brick rubble, and being made to pull these heavy carts to a place where they were building warehouses, or as the Japs called them, go-downs. He was on this work for quite a long time, and remembered with some upset the beatings he took at this time; he told me like many have before, it did not matter what you were doing, even if you were working as hard as you could, if one of the guards took a dislike to you, or you were the nearest to him, when he felt like hitting out at someone then it was you that caught the full force of his hatred. You learned to roll into a ball, and try to protect yourself; if you were one of the lucky ones you lived to tell the tale, if not, you died from the beating, even if not straight away – you may have taken so much damage to your body's vital organs, that you died the next day or in some cases even after several days of receiving a beating. Robert lost many of his best mates like this, and he told me there is not a day goes by that you don't think of them, and see them in your mind taking that beating.

After months of hard work with very little food, disease was breaking out in all the camps around Singapore; many of the men wounded in those last few days of the fighting had not made it, and Robert found himself attending many a best mate's funeral, after a hard days work. It was at this time that many of the men were being moved off to Japan to be used as forced labour in the mines and factories, but they had been told that they were being taken there to be put into proper Red Cross camps, where they would be cared for by doctors and nurses; many of the men believed this, only when they found themselves being thrown into the holds of Japanese cargo ships did they realise that they had been lied to again by the Japanese; on the trip to Japan many of them died, for they were given no water – the Japanese just used to pull back the door of the hold and throw water over them. The heat was unimaginable to us that have never been in the tropics, and if the Japanese guards showed any mercy to them at all it was by putting the hose pipe on them as they lay in the hold of the ship; the only trouble was that it was sea water that they hosed them with and it came at them with such high pressure that it killed many of them, but it made good amusement for the Jap guards. Some of the men who were lucky enough to survive this treatment have shared their stories with me and they will feature in my next book.

But for Robert life was turning bad now he was suffering bouts of malaria, and he had very bad dermatitis – so bad that the British medics knew he needed treatment urgently, so they asked for a Japanese doctor to look at him. Robert was kept at Changi prison hospital and the Japanese left him for a week before a doctor saw him; when the doctor did come to see him, he told Robert, through an interpreter, that he would be sending him to a proper Red Cross camp in Thailand where he would be cared for, and assured him that his dermatitis would soon get better once he arrived. About a week later Robert and many of his mates were marched off to the railway station where they were loaded into cattle trucks, with metal sides. Like many others, Robert remembered the burns he received to his arms when they touched the sides of the truck, which did his dermatitis no good at all. He soon realised that there would be no Red Cross camp for him for he knew by now what to expect from the Japanese; he told me how his mates helped him to survive the trip, and of how many of the men were not so lucky and did not survive the trip. After five days and nights in these cattle trucks they arrived at Ban Pong and soon saw that it was to be no picnic, there were no huts completed, and they all had to sleep up to their waists in mud as the rains had set in. There was hardly any food and morale was very low indeed at this time; the first thing the men did was to bury their dead, that had not survived the journey – many of Robert's mates from his Regiment were among the dead and he did his best to help see that they received a proper send off.

After a couple of days at Ban Pong Robert was moved on again and he told me how sorry he felt for those left behind in this stinking hell hole. After another forced march through virgin jungle, and trips on old barges up the river, he arrived at Wampo bridge where he was put to work on cutting down trees to use on the bridge building. As they cut down the trees the elephants dragged them away driven on by the little Malay boys sitting astride their heads. On one occasion one of the Jap guards did not think Robert was working hard enough, so he lashed out at Robert with his bamboo pickle stick; as he was lashing out at Robert one of the elephants brushed close by to the guard and Robert felt sure the elephant could sense that he was being ill treated. Many of us have heard the saying that an elephant never forgets, and Robert found this to be true, for some days later, this same guard was handing out another beating to one of the prisoners, when all of a sudden, this same elephant rushed at the guard knocking him down to the ground, and crushing the guard to death as he lay there, there was nothing the young Malay boy could do to stop it and once the elephant had killed this guard, it just turned away, and went back to collect more trees. Robert and the others stood in shock, for it had all happened so quickly, the other guards did not dare strike out at the elephant, and work ceased for a while as the guards ordered their friend's body to be taken back to camp – the young malay boy was taken along as well, and once away from the elephant he received a beating for what his elephant had done to the guard. For Robert and his mates it meant extra food that night, for once the Jap guard had been buried, the other guards laid food and items to help their departed comrade make his journey into the next world – Robert told me how he must have gone hungry on his journey for he and his mates soon had the food off the grave as soon as it turned dark; I can only imagine that next day when the other guards looked at the grave they must have felt that their friend had taken the food they had left for him. From then on the Jap guards did not hand out beatings while any of the elephants were about, which needless to say saved a lot of lives at that time.

The Japanese engineers worked the men very hard at this time for they needed the bridge built so badly to be able to get their troops up to Burma; gangs of men were kept busy pile driving the teak trees that Robert and his mates cut down into the river bed, others would tie the support members across and bind them up with thick tree creeper that they cut from the jungle, others would hammer in the steel spikes to hold it all together. To keep work going, the Japs set up acetylene lights so that the men could work into the night, and this was beginning to tell on the men. Tropical illness was taking a strong hold now and this was now the main cause of death, other than beatings. Robert by now was having to learn to live with his dermatitis, as were thousands of the others, and the only thing to relieve it was to bath in the river when you could – the river was the main life of the camp, providing all water, which had to be boiled first if possible, but this was not always possible, and so dysentery struck at an alarming rate, with most of the men living with it all the time.

Robert was soon moved on from Wampo as he was now to weak to manage the hard work involved. He was not lied to this time, no tales of going onto a Red Cross camp, he was just told to line up and be ready to leave. Once they were all lined up, Robert found that most of the men were from the 5th Norfolks; the Japs then did their usual trick of leaving them to stand in the full heat of the sun for three or four hours, before marching them off. It was a very long march as it was still late 1943, and the railway was just in its early days. They were going through virgin jungle a lot of the time, and this was just too much for many of them; they were just not in a fit state for such a trip.

As Robert told me of this time we shared a tear together as we remembered those of his friends that he had to leave in the jungle, for as you will know by now the Japs were very cruel, and those who could not keep up the guards soon bayoneted to death. Robert told me how when you saw this happening you found some strength from somewhere to keep going. On this march, food was scarce so they had to live off of the jungle, – fish from the rivers, snakes, monkeys, anything that they could catch they were glad to eat, but once again they could not boil the water and it was this that cost many of the men their lives, for it carried so many germs and soon crippled them up in pain, and when they could not keep up, there was always that guard ready with his bayonet. The only time the men got some rest was when they came to another camp, but then it was only for about a day – but it was a boost to them to be able to talk to the other prisoners in these camps, and exchange stories with them, mostly about the cruelty handed out by the guards.

After weeks of travelling like this Robert and the others that had survived reached Takanun, where after one nights sleep they were put straight to work on clearing the virgin jungle around them, and start building the camp. That night they were given tents to put up for them to sleep in – each tent held twenty six men, and Robert and his mates put them up with the thought of if nothing else it would keep the mosquitos off them, for you can imagine how many there were of them in this virgin jungle, but they soon found out that with twenty six men in a tent it got too hot, and they just had to open up the ends of the tents to let some air circulate through, but as soon as they did there were the mosquitos ready to eat them alive. The work was very hard as they had to now break through a large rock face some 30ft high and about a 300 yards long; the men were split into twos and were given a large chisel about a meter long, and one club-type hammer; they were suspended by rope from the top, and while one man held the chisel the other had to hit at it, they had to do at least one of these one meter long holes a day or they knew what they would receive, once the holes were done the Jap engineers put in the dynamite charges and set the fuses, they then usually picked the weakest prisoner to set light to the fuses while they stood well out of the way. On many occasions they would set some short fuses, and take bets among themselves as to whether the prisoner would be able to get away in time. Needless to say, more times then not he did not make it. Robert told me how after a time you just got used to their sick ways, and he remembered his friends that he had to bury in bits and pieces, and of how at first it made him sick, but as he told me, when death is all around you, you begin to accept it, and all you could do was hope and pray that you were not the unlucky one.

Robert knew now that if he did not get a break soon he would not make it for much longer, so one morning as he lined up in his work party, the Jap camp sergeant called out for smiths (meaning blacksmiths) to work the forge and make chisels. Robert knew enough to do this and so he stuck his hand up, the Jap sergeant pulled him out of the line, and one of the guards marched him over to the forges where he was given the meter long 1" thick round metal bars to sharpen the ends into chisels. He knew if he hung back the Japs would know that he knew nothing about being a smithy, so he got straight into it as if he had been doing it all his life. He got through that first day, and knew that this would save him if he could keep out of trouble and stick at it, he even found that the guard watching over them was not too bad, and some days he would slip them a banana as he walked by their forge. Robert had just over a week at this work, and he told me how it saved his life at that time, for it gave him time to rest up his tired out body, but then one day three men came to his forge to have their axes and chisels sharpened up – the Jap guard had told the men to go one at a time but they had all slipped off together. When the guard saw this he stormed over to where they were with Robert, and lashed out at them with his bamboo pickle stick, hitting them round the face – he even gave Robert one as well, then he turned and went to walk away, Robert vented his feelings by muttering what he thought of the guard, but unfortunately for Robert the guard could speak English, and he turned round and hit Robert again full in the face, which nearly took Robert's eye out; as he kept lashing out at Robert some of the other guards came over and joined in and after what seemed like a life time to Robert, he went unconscious. The others assumed he had been killed, and when the guards finally stopped kicking out at him, the Jap guards told them to take him away, and bury him, but as they did one of the lads felt a pulse, and knew that he was still alive; they took him to his tent, and laid him out, and did what they could for him, and said to one another if he makes it through the night he might have a chance. With their help Robert made it through the night, and the other lads kept him hidden for a day or two until he felt a bit better, for they knew if the guards saw him in this weak state they would only finish him off. They nursed him through this bad time, and saved his life. It is not hard for me to imagine why these Far Eastern prisoners of war have such great comradeship for they have all been to hell and back and lived to tell the tale, but as many of you know it is only now after 50 years on that many of them are starting to talk about it.

While Robert was laid up through his injuries one of the men in his tent died of cholera. He was Corporal Hornigold, Robert's Section Commander and was the first to die of cholera at Takanun; this frightened the Japs so much that they did not dare go near Robert's tent and it was this that helped the others to keep Robert out of the way until he recovered from his beating. The men left in Robert's tent were now ordered to keep away from the others, for fear of the cholera, and they were given the job of clearing jungle at the outskirts of camp, where they made the camp cemetery, and built the funeral fires to burn those that died from cholera. Their first one was for their dear friend Corporal Hornigold, and Robert told me how all the other twenty four men with him, and Robert himself, stood with tears running down their faces, as they stood and watched their friend's body burn away; they tried to comfort one another by saying "at least he is free now, the Japs can't hurt him any more." One of the men gave a prayer for his family back home, and for his beloved county of Norfolk. It was a great loss for all of them to bear, and no one replaced Corporal Hornigold in the tent, and in the next few weeks cholera took a firm hold and Robert and his mates where kept busy burning the bodies of those dear departed friends.

Robert told of how he can never forget the look on the faces of the dead mens' bodies as their muscles contracted in the heat of the fire, they would sit up and look at you – a sight that Robert still sees in his mind most days, for many of these men were Robert's friends. I remembered my own dear late father telling me the same thing, and Robert and I sat for a while as we got our emotions back in check.

Many of the men with Robert in this work party went down with cholera themselves, and Robert soon found that there was only now about fifteen of them left in his tent to perform the burials, and build the funeral fires; after each fire had burnt out they dug shallow trench graves and put all the ashes into them, they then made note of all the mens' names that they had burned, and made their own grave markers. One day while doing this work Robert just collapsed – yes, he to had now got cholera. It struck so quickly – you could feel alright in the morning and by night you had dropped dead from it; Robert's mates got him to their tent, for there was no proper hospital hut, as the camp was still being built. One of the medical boys gave him potash, the purple crystals which was all they had to help him, but Robert was one of the lucky ones, and he survived to face another day; he told me how he owed so much to his dear pals who cared for him at that time. Once he recovered he was sent back down the line to Chungkai hospital camp. It was while he was here that he met Bert who as you will recall was given the job of killing the buffalos, and when he brought the buckets of blood into the hospital hut, there lay Robert – it done them both the world of good to be able to talk of home together and think back to those happy childhood days. The cooks would let the blood congeal and then cook it as liver; Robert received his share of this, and soon started to pick up a little; he was given the job of gardening for the Japanese camp officers and he was pleased at last to be left to go at his own pace; he was also able to get a bit of extra food which at this time was a godsend to him; he told me how he remembered while laying in the hospital hut, how men had brought in food to help them; these men had risked their lives to get this food by slipping out of camp to barter with the natives, or to steal it from them; Robert told me how it was men like this that kept many of the chaps alive, and while he worked in the Japs garden Robert did his bit to get extra food for the sick hut.

After a few weeks of this light work, the Japs soon knew that he was as fit as any of the other prisoners, and Robert found himself being moved back up the line in a full work party, even though they all weighed about seven stone each now, they were now the fit ones, but as Robert said 'thank god they were taken in trucks', for if they had been force marched again, he did not think any of them would have made it. The trucks they travelled in this time were open top trucks, and as the trains were burning just wood in their boiler, the sparks blew straight into the trucks onto the men, which kept them from getting any rest, for fear of getting burnt. Their trip did not take too long and they soon arrived at Tamarkan were they were told they were to work on the bridge; before they were allowed into camp, they were all sprayed with disinfectant for such was the fear the Japs had of catching cholera; the guards took great delight in letting them know that here at Tamarkan they were very strict, and they handed out a beating to one poor chap just as a warning to them all of what to expect if they did not salute every Japanese guard and officer. There was to be no singing or whistling, no lectures, and no games or books; any one found doing or having any of these things would be put to death. As they helped their friend up after his beating, they said to one another 'what a welcome.' The heat of the day soon dried out the disinfectant on them, and left like a white powder all over them, which did Robert's dermatitis no good at all. It was now mid-afternoon, and all Robert and the others wanted was to be shown which hut they were in, and have a rest up – but no such luck they were taken straight away to join a work party at the bridge, where they were handed over to some of the cruelest guards they had met so far. None of them remembered to bow as they were handed over to these new guards, and sure enough all hell let loose; the guards all kicked out at them and knocked them to the ground and after some ten minutes of this treatment they were left to get up. Out of the twenty men only seventeen got up – yes, the others had been kicked to death. Robert and those left alive were then forced to stand to attention and look up at the sun, if they closed their eyes or looked down, they were beaten again; they were left like this for the rest of that day, until they were marched back to camp with all the other prisoners. Over the next few weeks Robert soon learnt to remember what the guards had told him the day he arrived, as he told me, he learnt the hard way.

After weeks of working on the bridge he was so ill with dysentery and beri beri that he could hardly walk, and so he was once again given the job of building the funeral fires, and the burning of the cholera victims. He was at an all time low now and thought that it would not be long before he probably caught it again and died himself, he felt so weak from the dysentery and when one of the medics told him to crush up some of the charcoal into ash and then take it with some water, Robert thought the medic was kidding him, but he tried it and once again lucky for him it worked – it helped settle his stomach. At last he kept some of the food in him, and started to feel better. He had to be so careful while working with the cholera victims, and did not dare touch his mouth with his hands. He washed down with the disinfectant, at the end of each day, and bathed in the river when allowed, but now the allied bombers were coming over, bombing the railway and the bridges, and Robert was taken from his cremation work, and found himself put into one of the travelling work parties to repair bomb damage to the railway; he travelled the length of the railway over the next year and saw some of the worst sights imaginable to man; he lived off rats, snakes and whatever they could catch and thought edible, they ate it. He told me that looking back at those times it is nothing but a miracle that he came through it all.

The Japanese interpreter with them now was not to bad to them, and he could speak perfect English; he told Robert one day that he had been born and brought up in America, and had gone for a holiday to see Japan in 1938 and while there he had been forced into the army; he took a lot of risks to help Robert and the others, sometimes he would slip one of them a note of how the war was going, which would be passed to the sergeant major to read; he also helped them with food from time to time. But then one day the Sergeant said to the lads 'our Interpreter friend as slipped me a note, and I want you all to listen carefully.' He then read it out as follows –

'atomic bombs dropped on Japan – no one alive.' Robert and the others could not believe it. Did it mean that everyone in Japan was dead? Their sergeant said we must carry on as usual, for if these guards think that all their home land is gone, they will just kill us for the sake of it; everyone worked on as usual and three days later a Jap guard came along the edge of the railway on a bike, and spoke to the interpreter, who then informed all of them they must return to the nearest main camp. The men hoped it was the news they had all dreamed of for so long, and they marched off along the railway line in twos back to camp. When they arrived at the camp all the other prisoners were just sitting on their bamboo platforms in their huts and they asked one another of what was going on. Robert and the others told them what they had heard through the interpreter three days ago. "Well something's afoot" said one of the men already at the camp, "these little yellow sods would not let us just sit about like this for nothing." Evening came, and the men turned in as usual – even if they could not sleep, as that eternal hope was now so strong in them – could they dare wish that it was now to be all over?

Robert told me that he thinks all of the men said a special prayer that night, and as he lay there thinking of home, he made a wish that his prayer would be heard and that he would soon be fit and well again, and back home with his loved ones. The night passed very slowly, and many of the men sat in groups talking. As sun up came, they had their rice ration, but still no work parties were called for and then at ten o'clock the sergeant was called for as he was their highest in command. He was marched to the Jap commandant and told that the Japanese had capitulated on their Emperor's orders, and that they would all now be set free; he asked the sergeant to tell the allies of how well they had all been cared for, at which the sergeant soon told him to remember all of the men that had been beaten and starved to death. The sergeant then turned away with out bowing, and marched back to inform the men; most of them were overcome with emotion and cried like babies; men hugged one another and cried their eyes out; some could not take it all in; others had heart attacks through the sheer excitement and died were they fell. The sergeant quickly brought them to order, and informed them to take care there was to be no reprisals, and they were to remember that the Japanese were still armed.

The men spent the rest of that day just relaxing and trying to take it all in; they had been prisoners for three and a half years, and most of them were in a shocking state. The next morning they awoke to find that the Japs had cleared out and left them alone, so they spent that day getting the sick ready to travel – those that could, would help carry anyone that could not walk with out help, and the next morning it was a sorry sight that left that camp, and marched their way along the railway line until they arrived at a camp where the allies were. Robert remembered then being taken by train to Bangkok were he stayed for two weeks until he was fit enough to fly to Rangoon hospital. He like many others asked the pilot if he would be safe, for he had never flown before; the pilot told him in his American brogue "you just sit there buddy, because after all you've been through this will be a treat." Robert took his word and sat back, and let them tie him to the side panelling for it had no proper seats to sit in, but the pilot was very good and flew as low as he could for he could see only too well the condition they were in.

Robert arrived at Rangoon Hospital where he stayed for two weeks, before boarding the Worcestershire to bring him home. After a wonderful trip he arrived off Liverpool in October 1945 and to see dear old England again was a tonic in itself. He thought back to the day he had sailed out of Liverpool all those years before, and of the hell he had been to, he thanked God for seeing him through, and he stood with a silent prayer for all those mates he had left behind in the jungles of Thailand, for he had lost all his close friends out there, and was the only one of them to return. Robert could not wait to get ashore and to set foot on dear old England again.

The crowds that had gathered were cheering so loudly and waving flags – it was such a wonderful sight for all the men. Robert was up to around eight stone now, and was soon sent from the transit camp with his train ticket for home. When he arrived back at Kings Lynn station his family and friends had gathered to meet him and there were plenty of tears of joy shed that day as they all gave thanks for his safe return. Robert attended many parties over the next few weeks, and he visited the families of his friends that had not been so lucky as him; he returned to Congham Hall for a week to help his old friends there plant a new orchard of apple trees, with the help of German prisoners of war. He thought to himself how lucky they were, and of how well treated and fed they all were – if only he could have been treated like it then perhaps all his friends would have come home with him.

Robert missed his mates very much, and when he received the offer of attending a new training course to learn new skills he went for it; he was taken round large factories, which was all new to him, and he decided that he would like to work with electronics, so this is what he applied for, only to be informed that there were only places for disabled people to learn about electronics. So instead he went to Letchworth training college to learn to be a bricklayer, but as time went on Robert returned to his first love back on the land – he took over a smallholding in Great Massingham where he still lives to day. He met his dear wife Doris in 1957 and with her help he worked hard and built up his farm. They were married in 1959 on June the 11th some 36 years ago. In 1977 Robert had a complete breakdown and spent a lot of time in psychiatric hospitals like Chatterton House near Kings Lynn and one in Woolwich. Doris told me how the doctors had told her that the human nervous system is not completely formed until you are about twenty five years old, and that the worst thing to affect it is malnutrition. Need we say any more of why these brave men have suffered with their nerves ever since they came home.

Robert came through it all with the help of his dear wife, but as she told me, she is just one of thousands that have helped keep their husbands sane, for it is always the wife who is there when their husbands nightmares return them to those dark days of death in those camps.

Robert and Doris have been back to Singapore and Thailand for, like many of the men, he wanted to see the places that he had suffered in, and as he is the only surviving Far Eastern prisoner of war in Great Massingham, he wanted to pay his respects to all those friends he had to leave out there; it was a very emotional moment for Robert as he laid his wreath on their war graves. Their dream is to return this year on the 50th anniversary of Victory over Japan.

Robert my thanks go to you for sharing your story with us, to you and Doris and for the thousands of couples like you, who gave so much for my today, I thank you.

God bless and keep you both, and may all your dreams come true.

Footnote

Robert told me that for the last eighteen months of his captivity, he had no boots or any kind of footwear at all, and so he had to work barefoot, which built up a layer of hard skin about half an inch thick on the bottom of his feet. Before the war he had suffered with terrible sweaty, feet which had been very embarrassing for him, but if nothing else it had cured his smelly feet.

Robert, I'm sure there must be easier ways to cure smelly feet.

Chapter Seven

LETTERS

I would like to share with you now, just some of the letters I have received from people who have had their lives affected, in some way, by the nightmares of those dark days of the 1940s. I have told you how I have shed many tears while talking to and writing my heroes' stories. In some way I feel I have put part of my life into that era of time, and I can assure you while writing the book I felt as if I was there with them. I shared their beatings and hardships with them and, yes, shed many a tear when my emotions ran high. But when my wife and I read these letters, I can tell you we both cried, for as you will see they are things that touch the heart. Perhaps I should send them to our Prime Minister to read – who knows, it might help in some way to get our boys that compensation they so richly deserve, for as you know I feel that our Government should make sure that all who survived at the hands of the Japanese should be on a 100% war pension, while they demand compensation from the Japanese.

For my own father and many many more men it is now to late, but I beg our Government to not leave it any longer for those still suffering on in their twilight years. They gave their all for our country, and answered their Government's call to serve, they have marked the paths of history and as that history shows us, they were thrown into a lost cause by the Government of the day – so let our today's Government show these men that are left just how much we appreciate what they gave for us to be here today, and what better time than now on this 50th anniversary year for them to be compensated, and as we remember the men please remember also all the poor women that were raped and abused at the hands of the Japanese guards. My heart goes out to them all. One thing I do know is that we should not repay these now senior citizens who gave their all for our today, by sticking VAT on their fuel bills and by making everything so expensive for them, when they only ever get a very small increase on their pensions. We see every day now how some poor old person may have to be moved from their home, because they or the council can not afford to keep them any more. Is this not a bad way for us to treat these people? Whatever must the rest of the world think of us? One thing my father did tell me about the Japanese is that they do care for their old people.

Enough of my own feelings. Let's now share the feelings of those people who wrote to me after reading my book "MY DAD MY HERO."

The first letter is from Mrs. H. Davie of Sidcup in Kent. She tells me......

Dear Mike

I was so moved at your Dad's life as a P.O.W. in the Far East that I just had to write to you. For you see, Michael, my own dear husband was also a FEPOW. His name was Bill Davie and he too worked on the death railway, and went right to the finish of the line, and finished up at three Pagoda pass, and was weighed in at 5 stone 4 lbs when the allies set him free. All our married life, thirty eight years, he was a very sick man because of it, but he was such a special man and I loved him so very much, and when he died eight years ago, my life felt like it had ended as well.

Bill did such a lot of good work for the London FEPOW Club and I was twenty years old when I joined as well, I still go to "TENKO" every month and I am now 69 years old, as FEPOWs are and always will be a special kind of men. I cannot find it in my heart to forgive the Japs for what they did to my Bill and all those other brave lads, I just hope God can forgive them. I am now living on a widows retirement pension, in a little flat, but I try to get on with life as best I can. The other FEPOWs are a great strength to me, and if you ever come to London please call and visit me.

I wish you all the best with the book, and thank you for what you are doing to help those still suffering.

Yours sincerely,
Hilda Davie.

Thank you, Hilda, for your letter. I know how much you miss your dear Bill. May God bless and keep you safe in your retirement.

From Mr. Ben Bingham of Hereford......

Dear Michael,

I thought you might like this photo of Changi barracks taken in 1942, to see for yourself how the Japs crammed the prisoners in. Also, as you will know, the Malay people are very small, in comparison to us, but there was this giant of a man, who stood 6' 8" tall, and when the Japs took Singapore, in the hand to hand fighting that took place, he actually killed two of them by picking them up, and smashing their heads together. But he could not fight off all of them single handed, and the other Japs took him prisoner. They then broke both his arms and legs, but to his fate they never killed him, but they never allowed his broken bones to be mended. He was left to crawl around and fend for himself best he could.

After the war when I met him, he was very badly disabled and distorted, yet he was proud enough to get a job sweeping the roads, at the married quarters at GHQ in Singapore. One day a three ton lorry went out of control, and a little girl was in its path, and this gentle giant of a man, badly distorted as he was, threw himself across

Changi prison during World War 2, originally for 3,000 men. The photograph shows 17,000 incarcerated there. The photo was used in the Japanese War Trials in1945.

the road to pick her up, and held her out at arms length, with his badly broken arms, to save her, and let the runaway truck hit him instead. He did survive, and the people on that married quarters knew from then on what a HERO they had among them.

Some School friends of mine were held in Changi prison, and a prison camp in Malaya, and one thing that always sticks in my mind is that when they were first interned, a large bowl of soup was supplied for them, the soup was covered in dead flies etc, and they spent quite a while scooping them out, but as time went on they were so hungry that they ate the flies as well.

I met a Peter Chung, a Chinese man, who told me how he had been forced to watch the deaths of two allied service men who were tied up with barbed wire and then had a hose pipe pushed down their throats, and the tap turned on until they were so full with water, that the barbed wire, punctured them, the hose pipes were then removed, and then he told me how the Japs took it in turn to run and jump on their stomachs until they burst open. He could not forget how the Japs then stood and laughed at the sight of the two men. They then bayoneted them in the heart to make sure they were dead; they had already dug their own graves, and Mr Chung told me how he and the others had to put them into their graves and bury them.

I hope you don't mind me sharing these things with you, Michael, but I think the world should know what these men did for our today and of what they suffered. Keep up the good work.

Yours sincerely,
Ben Bingham.

Dear Ben: Thanks so much for your letter and your kindness in sending me the photo. As you say in your letter, we must all pray such things never happen again.

My thanks to Mrs. Joyce Martin of Kent, for her kindness in loaning me her photos of Singapore, taken from her late uncles collection.

Her uncle served in the Royal Navy and was a man I would dearly liked to have met to share his stories. His first ship was H.M.S. Benbow shown in the photo below in 1927. He was a full time sailor and saw the world many times over. He visited Singapore before the war and the second picture shows H.M.S. Kent being refuelled in Singapore Naval Base in 1930; little did he know then of the action he was to see in the years to come.

Orchard Road, Singapore, where the Japanese Kempei-Tai tortured many of our men as well as local Chinese and Malays, etc.

Our boys would have lived in huts similar to these.

Outside the city the people led a primitive life.

Our next letter is from Mr. E Maxwell of Kelbrook, Lancashire.......

Dear Mr. Bentinck

Please forward me a copy of your book "MY DAD MY HERO." I heard you talking about it on Radio Lancashire and I must admit it had me in tears. My wife's brother-in-law was one that suffered on the death railway, and he could never bring himself to talk about it to us, as he would just say it was too horrific. Like your dad, he weighed 4 stone when the allies got to him, he suffered ill health for the rest of his life because of what he went through for us all, and after all he had been through he was knocked down by a car two years ago and died from his injuries. For him his suffering finished that day, but we will never forget him and of what he gave for our today.

Yours affectionately

E. Maxwell.

Letter from Mr. D. Mc Dermott, Manchester........

Dear Mr. Bentinck

I have just read your article in the Manchester Evening News, about your book, and concerning men who were in the war in the Far East. I would like to order a copy please.

My father was out there. He was in the Royal Artillery and was in Malaya when the Japs invaded, and the last my mother heard of him was a telegram from Singapore dated 3-2-42 saying he was OK and not to worry. She never heard another word for 2 years when she received word that my father was missing, presumed dead, and that he had been mentioned in dispatches, and that she would receive his medal with the Oak leaf.

He is buried under the monument at Kranchi war cemetery in Singapore. My father's home town is Chesterfield Derbyshire. Please, if you find any of the ex FEPOWs that you speak to knew my father, please, please ask them to contact me to let me know how he died, for I would like to know, for you see I never knew my father, and he never knew that mum was expecting me when he sailed off to fight for his country.

Yours thankfully,
Dick Mc Dermott.

Dear Dick: Thank you so much for writing to me. What can I say? Your dear father gave his tomorrow for our today, and although we can never repay him or any of them for what they gave for us, we must let people know of what they went through for us to be here today. At least I knew my dear father, and my heart goes out to you, for I know it has not been easy for you. I have notified the Far Eastern Prisoners Of War Association, of your request and they will notify their members, and I pray that one of them is still alive that knew your father, and can help you with all you want to know. God bless you and your family.

Letter from Mr. & Mrs S. Chown of Cambridge........

Dear Mr. Bentinck.

My husband was also a FEPOW out there on the death railway, with F. force, apparently the worst of the lot, all the way to Burma border camp Sonkrai. Actually he thinks he knew your father. Prior to being moved up country, he was in charge of two kitchens (as he was a chef). He had been the chef in Changi cooking for the R.A.M.C. and for the Cambridgeshires. He has had men in Cambridge who he did not know come up to him and say to him 'you saved my life, and I would like to thank you for that, and shake your hand.'

To him they had been one of a number of men he had tried to help, and if he could he would find them a job in the kitchen where he could look out for them until they had recovered; he saved many of them by making up various dishes, made from cats, rats, snakes, etc and all sorts of rice dishes. He still loves a rice pudding but it

Above: Mr. Chown still cooks a cake every year for his Regiment's Dinner and does all the decorations himself.
Left: A menu for P.O.W.s in Karanji Hospital hut. Although there was only fish and rice, Mr. Chown made all he could from it to cheer the men up. The water he bottled and made up names and told them to pretend it was wine.

must have plenty of milk with it, not like they got it in the camps.

He has many books on the war and would like to add your book to his collection, and he believes that talking about what he went through helps him, as after all it was one of the main parts of their lives. He has his share of nightmares, as he remembers that many of the escapees had letters on them for me, I always hoped and prayed that he would come home, but if the allies had not dropped the H. Bomb I know things would have been different.

One chap my Stan helped had lost his arm, when the Prince of Wales was sunk, and Stan helped get him a job in the kitchens with him; he was so pleased as he realised this probably saved his life at the time, that he asked Stan if he could grant him any wish he would do his best to make it come true. Stan knew that this chap had been an artist, and so he asked him to paint him a picture of me, for Stan had hidden a small photo that I had given him, and from this the chap did a painting of me for Stan, on stolen paper from the Japs – the brush was made from hairs from his head, and paint was from blood and any crushed thing that gave colour.

The Australians presented Stan with a scroll (shown below) for what he had done to help them, and all the officers in the camp signed it, Stan knew if the Japs found any of these it would be his lot, so he hollowed out a piece of bamboo and hid them all inside it, and then buried the bamboo some-where safe. My Stan and all those brave lads suffered so much. Stan lost 7 stone in body weight, but as he says, he was one of the lucky ones, for he came home. He is now 83 years old and has had his share of suffering over the years, from the things he went through out there, but at least we have had a life together. One never forgets those brave chums that did not make it, and not a day goes by that we don't give thanks for what they gave for our today.

Yours most sincerely,
Mrs. D.E. Chown.

Mr. Chown was presented with the M.B.E. for his services to catering. He was in the 196 Field Ambulance R.A.M.C. and saved many lives with his cooking and care of them.

Dear Mr. & Mrs. Chown: Your letter speaks for itself – yes, of a brave man, for I have spoken to many FEPOWs who have told me what you did for them Stan. Many of them have mentioned how, as they lay in the hospital hut that they called the death hut, they had accepted in their mind that their time had come, only to find that someone was trying to get them to drink or eat some special type of food to help get some life saving vitamins into them. It's thanks to you Stan, even if it was rats, cats, snakes, etc – you made time for them and prepared the best you had for them, and those who survive today will never forget you or be able to thank you enough. On their behalf I thank you now for your love and care of these brave brave men. God bless you. I know how privileged my wife and I are to be able to have you and your dear wife as our friends. We know we can never repay you for what you gave for our today but we are only to pleased to try.

Letter from Mrs. M. Balshaw of Bacup, Lancashire.......

Dear Sir,

Please send me one of your books. I think it is very good work you are doing in letting people know of what these brave men did for us, and of the terrible things they suffered in the death railway camps. My sister's husband died working on the death railway, and left two lovely little girls aged 2 and 5 years old; it was many years before my sister got to know the whereabouts of the cemetery where the memorial stone that carries his name has been erected. She was never able to visit the place, but worked hard to bring her girls up to respect the memory of their dad. I think a lot of things have been kept in the dark for far to long and we pray that through your books that people will learn by it and never let such things happen again.

Yours faithfully,

Mrs M. Balshaw.

Letter from Mrs. P. Winter of Beeston, Nottingham.......

Dear Mr Bentinck,

I wonder if you can help me find out what my dad went through as a prisoner of the Japanese in the second world war. I know he was put into Changi prison when he was 25 years old, but I don't know when he became a prisoner, as he would never talk about any of it to us. When he died the doctor told us what he had gone through made sure he did not make old age. Mum told us how much weight he had lost as a prisoner of the Japs and we could hardly believe it. My dad was in the R.E.M.E. and his name was Kenneth Charles Bathmaker. I think he lived in Hackney, London until he joined the R.E.M.E. My brother and sister and me now know what our dad must have gone through, and we feel very proud to be able to say our dad was a FEPOW. If you can help me to find anyone still alive who might have known my dad please can you write to me and let me know.

Dear Pauline: You will have received my letter by now of how I have set things in motion, to find anyone who knew your dad, but perhaps someone will read your letter here and make contact. Please don't feel that your dad did wrong by not telling you about what he went through, for as you now know he probably found it to horrific to talk about, like many of these brave men do, but like all these men he will always be a HERO to me. Take care of your Mum. God bless and keep you and your family.

Our next letter is from Mrs. C. Peachey of Wisbech, Cambs.......

Dear Mr. Bentinck,

I have just been listening to you on radio Norfolk and would like a copy of your book. My late husband was in the 2nd Cambs and was also a prisoner of the Japs like your father; he had been in the T.A. so he was in from the start of the war – he always considered himself very lucky to have come home, and for those first few years we had many long silent walks, but as time went on he was able to talk a little about the bad times, as well as of the way they all supported one another, and made the best of a very bad job. He would have liked to have gone back to visit Singapore, but although compared to some he had relatively good health apart from a nervous breakdown during his working years, his health deteriorated quickly after his retirement, so that ambition was never realised.

Although he had lost his sight and was not walking well, he reached his "three score and ten" before he died 12 years ago; he also lived to see our oldest grandson in his naval uniform before he lost his sight and was a memory he treasured.

The Singapore Club of FEPOWs still goes on in Wisbech although the numbers are dwindling fast, but there is still that strong bond of comradeship among them, and few people except them can really know what they went through. There is a special memorial in St Peter's Church, Wisbech – perhaps your dear late father was one of the large congregation who came to the impressive dedication service all those years ago.

Thank you for what you are doing to repay these brave men for your life today – I wish you good luck with your second book and good luck always.

Yours sincerely
Connie Peachey.

P.S. Michael, as you will know, today is the 15th of February and 50 years today that Singapore fell, I think our St Peter's Church will have Singapore orchids on the memorial, that the FEPOW club have had flown in. Bye.

Dear Mrs. Peachey: Thank you for being one of those dear wives who have cared and helped these brave men to make the best of their lives. I know you are just one of thousands who have helped their husband to get through their nightmares – to you and all the widows I say thank God for our FEPOW clubs, and thank God your husbands had you.

Letter from Mrs. I. Lambourne of Northampton.......

Dear Mr Bentinck

I heard you on Radio Northampton discussing your book and was so moved to hear how much your poor father suffered at the hands of the Japanese. My husband was on air sea rescue and was down to be posted to Singapore in 1941, but shortly before he was due to go, he had an accident and broke his leg badly; another poor man had to replace my husband on the posting. Although he was never able to trace his replacement, he now realises that he broke his leg at a lucky time for himself; he is now 81 and he would dearly love to read your book and to know of your brave father's story. We thank you for what you are doing to help these men, who are still suffering today.

Thanking you in anticipation,
Yours sincerely
Iris Lambourne

Letter from Mr. R. Bluxam. of March, Cambs.......

Dear Michael,

I was very lucky to catch your radio interview on Radio Norfolk, and to hear the fascinating and moving account of your father's war-time experiences. I was a fighter pilot, with the British pacific fleet and my carrier was part of the task force sent into Hong Kong to take the Japanese surrender. Being then with out a useful role, we pilots were put ashore and given various tasks in helping to restore order, from utter chaos. My particular job was to supervise a large working party of Japs who were now our prisoners, we had to clear out and clean blocks of flats in Kowloon to prepare them as temporary accommodation for British P.O.W.s. prior to their repatriation. I remember only too well the shock of seeing that first batch of returning P.O.W.s. (from Shanghai, I think) – they were in such a distressing state.

I suspect that many a story has gone untold by ex FEPOWs simply because to recall them in fine detail becomes too harrowing for those concerned. Congratulations therefore on your diligence in preparing publication of your book, from your dad's records and from what he shared with you while he lay ill in hospital – a brave man indeed. I look forward to reading my copy and will be making it known to several ex-service friends. Keep up your good work.

Yours sincerely,

Richard Bluxam.

Letter from Mrs. M. E. Watson Nottingham.......

Dear Mr. Bentinck

I felt I must write to you a few lines, after hearing you on Radio Nottingham – it was so interesting also very emotional for me. My husband was in the Sherwood Foresters, and was taken prisoner at the fall of Singapore, and was in Changi prison and on the death railway. I think he knew your father when they were at River Valley Camp – he weighed around 5 stone when he was released and had all the usual things when he got home – he suffered with nervous trouble from that day on. He died 12 years ago in May.

We had been to the Cambridge FEPOWs Yasume club with the Nottingham FEPOWs, where we had lunch and met old friends that my Frank had met in those death railway camps. We had a lovely day with them all, but on the way home on the coach, Frank collapsed and died in seconds. He was in his mid sixties. I was with 50 other FEPOWs and their wives and they all shared in my loss with me, and it was these people who helped me through. We had one son who was in the police and one night a year ago he came home after being on nights, and went to bed never to wake up again – he was just 44 years old. The hurt and the pain will not go away, but I do have two lovely grandchildren, two smashing Grandsons of 16 and 20 years old. I also have a wonderful daughter-in-law; she is so very kind to me. I am so lucky to have them and they are now my life and what I live for.

Frank used to say that all FEPOWs wives should receive a medal for how they have cared for their men, but we know that love conquers all. I hope you don't mind me sharing my troubles with you, and I do thank you and your wife for what you are doing for our FEPOWs. Bless you.

Yours Sincerely,

Margaret E Watson.

Dear Margaret: May I be so informal? I know by now that I can because we have written to one another a few times since I received your first letter printed above. My wife and I both cried when we read your letter, and I must admit I cried again when writing it out for the book – you are one brave lady Margaret. I know you will always have your memories of Frank and your dear son, and I know how you treasure them, but Frank and your son are now in a far better place, and they are together. Our Lord said I go to prepare a place for you, and I know how much Frank suffered in life at the hands of the Japanese, and I am sure our Lord has a special place for all our brave FEPOWs, at his right hand side. Take care, Margaret – face that world full on always with a smile, and boys – keep looking after Gran. God bless you all.

Letter from Mrs. M. Chadwick, Manchester.......

Dear Sir,

I would like a copy of your book. My husband William was a prisoner of the Japs and suffered for the rest of his life. 'He came home' was all he would say. He was an invalid for 45 years but I managed to look after him until he died. I am now in a warden-controlled flat, but they look after me best they can, but I miss my husband for he like all FEPOWs was a special man.

Yours Sincerely,

Mrs May Chadwick.

Letter from Mrs. A. Richardson, Lincoln.......

Dear Mr. Bentinck

I really enjoyed listening to you talk on Radio Lincoln yesterday. I would like a copy of your book as it will be of great interest to me, as my uncle, who died last year, was in Changi prison and was used as slave labour. Like your father he didn't talk about his ordeal until the very end when he told my father many stories, mainly to get them off his chest, I think. I find it very sad that men such as your father and my uncle Norman had to bottle up so many horrific things throughout their lives. I hope your book is a great success and the help you are giving to the surviving FEPOWs is swift, as they have lived with promises from governments for the last 50 yrs. so keep up your good work.

Yours faithfully,

Angela Richardson.

From Mr. R. Elliott, Lincoln.......

Dear Mr. Bentinck

Please send me a copy of your book about your late fathers experiences as a Japanese POW that I heard you talking about on Radio Lincoln, on Melvin Prior's programme. It was just so moving. I am only 47 years old so was not around at that dreadful time, but it is a subject I feel extremely strong about, having been in the R.A.F. and heard how they treated airmen. I refuse to buy anything Japanese and often tell my children why. I hope they will read the book and I wish you every success with it. Please put the bit extra to your FEPOW funds.

Yours faithfully,

Richard Elliott.

From Mr. G. Crisp, Essex......

Dear Mr. Bentinck

I am writing to tell you just how much I enjoyed your book. It helped me to realise just how much these brave men went through, and of what they gave up or lost. Even though I believe we should look to the future and not dwell on the past, I believe that a valuable lesson can be learned from the terrible things that so called civilized people have done to each other. My own father was one of the first into Belsen when it was liberated by the allies. I understand from my mother that the things he saw there changed him, he never forgot and I'm sure that he found it hard to forgive. Also his health suffered and the illness he caught in the camp was a factor in his death, a few years ago. Even though I enjoyed your book I found it profoundly sad that humans can inflict all that unnecessary pain and suffering on to fellow humans. Please let me know when your new book is ready and thanks for all your efforts in helping these HEROES.

Yours Sincerely,
Geoff Crisp.

From Mr. G. Taylor, Hampshire

Dear Mr. Bentinck,

Thanks for the book – once I started it I could not put it down. Even knowing what I do about the Japanese I found some of the incidents chilling to say the least and your father must have been made of such great stuff, with guts and spirit to survive it all. I must congratulate you on putting it into a book for us all to know about, and for lasting evidence. There has been much talk lately about us showing the hand of friendship to the Germans and Japanese, and I might go along with that if they had publicly admitted their guilt and paid some handsome recompense to their victims. My local Vicar holds a service on the foreshore each year to honour the dead of Hiroshima but few people attend as he never mentions the

FEPOWs or the poor murdered nurses. I only served in India & Burma but I saw enough to know what the FEPOWs suffered. Thanks for what you are doing for them.

Yours sincerely,
Geoff Taylor.

Letter from Mrs E. Stupples, Lincolnshire.......

Dear Mr. Bentinck

I have read your book twice and have now passed it to a friend. How can one express the feelings it aroused? Impossible. It must have been a great relief for you to get all those thoughts down on paper that your dear father had shared with you. The comradeship between those suffering men was unbelievable. I know each generation brings its own problems and each person deals with theirs in their own way. Yes your dad really was a Hero.

Yours Sincerely,
Eileen Stupples.

Letter from Susan Rhodes. Maldon Essex.

Dear Mr. Bentinck.

I hope you did not mind me ringing you the other evening, it was great to talk to you, for when I heard you speaking on radio Essex the other afternoon, I could have listened for hours to you speaking. I had just picked up my boys aged 12 and 14 from school and we all sat in the car listening to you on our way home. I was in tears at the anguish your dear dad must have gone through, and how privileged you must have felt at him opening his heart to you. My boys and I very much look forward to reading our copy of the book, as you say you chose the right title what else could you have called it but MY DAD MY HERO.

Yours with kindest regards,
Mrs. Susan Rhodes.

Photos of the Japanese surrender in Singapore. Taken on 12th September 1945 by Mr. James Stuart, ex Chief Petty Officer who was given the job of guarding the Japanese Officers on their surrender. Sent to me by his nephew, Alastar MacBean from Cheshire.

Lord Louis Mountbatten arrives at the City Hall.

R.A.F. Flying boats fly-past.

Crowd at Singapore City Hall waiting for the Japanese to arrive.

Japanese Generals entering City Hall to sign the surrender document.

Letter from Mrs. L. Grey, Kent.......

Dear Mr. Bentinck,

I heard your talk on London News talk last night about your father's diaries. I was very moved to hear about his experiences at the hands of the Japanese. I am sure there must be many people like your father who never got over their experiences, but if by publishing his account it can at least make people stop and think, and perhaps make a more determined effort to be more humane to fellow human beings, he will in his own way have achieved something. Best of luck with the book.

Yours wishing you every happiness,
    Mrs. L. Grey.

.Letter from Jennifer Jones, London.......

Dear Mr. Bentinck,

I heard you talking to Jeremy Dry on London News Talk last night (Jeremy gave me your address). I too have listened with horror to my father, relating stories similar to the ones you were speaking about, as he too was a Japanese P.O.W. and was fed on a small cup of rice for those 3 years. He was sent to Japan and forced to work in the mines, (among other things). My father is still with us but suffers ill health, Parkinson's Disease being the main culprit; I would love to take him to the Far East this year, but fear his health would not be up to it, as like most of our brave FEPOWs they alone really know the suffering.

I wish you well with the book.

Yours sincerely,
    Jennifer Jones.

Letter from Mr. A. Clark, Stockton on Tees, Cleveland.......

Dear Mr. Bentinck,
    I heard you last night on Bob Roberts Programme on Radio North, and would like your book. My Grandfather was captured at Singapore and would only talk about the nicer side of his experiences such as signing their names as Mickey Mouse, Donald Duck etc on the forms that the Japanese wanted them to fill in, and of the time he and a friend had been volunteered to make a garden for the camp commandant and just as their hard work had begun to bare fruit, they were moved on to begin work on the death railway. As I was only 17 years old when he died I think that his refusal to talk to me about that episode in his life, was because he felt that I was too young to understand or to believe the horrors of that time. I want to read your book to help me know more of what my Grandfather and his comrades did for me; please let me know of any other books you have written or books that you can recommend, to help me know more on the subject. Thanking you in anticipation, keep up the good work.
    Yours faithfully,
    Andy Clark.

Dear Andy: I know I can not answer all the letters, or the book will be too big and become too expensive, but Andy I must answer yours. It pleases me so much when someone as young as you wants to know more about these brave men; your Grandfather was one of a special breed of men the likes we will never see again. They alone probably are the only ones to know what the word suffering really means, along with the Jews in Europe. I know your Grandfather would be so proud of you, and your letter tells me of your love for him. I hope you find the list of book titles I have sent you will help you find out why I hold these men in such high esteem. I know you will have read this book by now, and assure you all the stories are true, so you see why they are such special men.
    Yours sincerely, Michael Bentinck.

Letter from Mrs. Brenda Ratcliffe, Suffolk.......

Dear Mr. Bentinck,

It was so nice to hear you on Radio Norfolk yesterday. I must admit I don't usually listen in at that time of day but I was waiting for a friend so I switched on while I waited. I'm so glad I did for I found your talk so moving. My brother-in-law worked on that death railway, but never speaks of it; he has never been a well man and he lost so many of his friends; he was in the Norfolk Regiment. It was so nice to hear you speak of your dad with so much love and respect – a very rare thing today. I can't wait to receive my book and wish you much success with it.

Yours sincerely,
Mrs. Brenda Ratcliffe

Letter from Frank Aldous, Bury St. Edmunds, Suffolk.......

Dear Mr. & Mrs. Bentinck,

Thanks for sending my book so quickly, and for the nice words you signed in the front for me. Your late father suffered some horrendous treatment as a FEPOW. He was lucky, as you say, to survive. I was fortunate that I did not work on the railway of death, but was sent to north Japan to work in a cement works. After 50 years it still seems like yesterday in my mind, and instead of 3 years as a prisoner it seems more like 35 years. We were very unfortunate, that the Japanese considered themselves superior to all other races, and they were also brutalised by a militarian regime. We were not P.O.W. but captives (Horiows). The 18th Division had a very raw deal in their war to defend Singapore as its fate was doomed by the time we arrived, without our full artillery and transport. Also the nips had complete naval and air control. I have always given thanks that I was spared to return to my beloved U K. Michael, your father was indeed a HERO.

All my best wishes,
Frank Aldous.

From Mr. B. Kirkham, age 38, Lancashire.......

Dear Mr. Bentinck.

I heard you on Radio Lancashire talking about your book and of what your dad had shared with you; it brought all the horrific stories back to me that my own father had told me about his imprisonment under the Japs, including Changi prison and the death railway, where he was at the camp near the bridge on the Kwai. Unfortunately, my father died suddenly of a heart attack in January 1994. Although after returning home from the Far East he spent a year in hospital, he led a very active life. My mother and myself both miss him so much but we are at present watching all the world at war programs, and programs about compensation from the Japanese. I know my father would have been glued to the TV, as all he ever wanted was to be recognised as a very badly treated FEPOW. compensation would be very nice and welcome, although as you said in your radio interview, just a simple but sincere apology a few years ago would have gone a long way towards helping my father to forgive if not forget. My father always deplored the treatment, not least from our own government. On receiving some of his many medals after the war he was staggered to find that he had to buy them, or at least the ribbons to hang them on, so that he could hang them from his chest; is this not another insult after spending five years away from home suffering in terrible conditions, to be told to buy your own medals. He often told me that when Singapore fell that there were many planes still in their crates on the harbour, as nobody had bothered to send anyone over to put them together. They once were told to line up on an airfield and salute the allies planes as they came over, although my father was a fieldgunner he knew from the silhouettes that they were Jap planes. The British soldiers were told they would be court marshalled if they did not hold their ranks. My father grabbed his mate and ran and jumped in a ditch; when they came out of it afterwards there were many laying dead, does this not show you that the officers knew very little. When Singapore fell my father was sent for more ammunition to get to the front lines; when he arrived for it he found it was officers party night, and whilst they were busy dancing no ammo could be released, as nobody would sign the release papers for it, meanwhile men at the front were having to fight hand to hand which, as I know that you know only too well, cost thousands of mens lives. He also told me it was a miracle that any of the men came back at all, as our officers where total plonkers most of the time, but he assured me there were exceptions to the rule, and that those exceptions were very brave men indeed – even if there was not many of them. If any of these things I mention are of use to you please make contact through me as my mother could probably tell you much more in greater detail. It's such a pity that my father is not here today as he would have loved to write to you and talk to you he was very proud to have been in the Blackpool Regiment 137 Royal Artillery. Gunner. J. KIRKHAM 950909. God rest his soul.

Yours,

Brian Kirkham – like you, a proud son of a brave FEPOW.

From Mrs. K. Raeburn, Cambridge.......

Dear Mr. Bentinck,

Please send me a copy of your book MY DAD MY HERO. I would like to give it to my son who has always been so interested because his uncle (my brother) was a prisoner of the Japs, and on arrival home in 1946 he underwent operations to try to put right his injuries that he suffered in the defence of Singapore. Sadly he died and there had to be a post mortem – the doctors at Addenbrooke's put gunshot wounds on the death certificate, and the doctor said to me "Mrs Raeburn, take consolation – I know his dearest wish would have been to see England again, with all it green fields and this by the grace of god was granted for a short time." My brother never talked to me about any of his experiences for I was his little sister, but my son did know his uncle and loved him dearly although he was only a small boy. I went to Waterstones but they had none of your books left – please put this right as everyone should know what these brave men did for us.

Yours sincerely,

Mrs. Kay Raeburn.

Letter from Mrs. P. Parker, Leicester.......

Dear Mr. Bentinck,

I was very interested to hear you talking on Radio Leicester, concerning the book you have written as a tribute to your late father. My husband was a FEPOW for 3 years and was also forced to work on the death railway, and was for a time in Changi prison. Like your father, he also does not talk about it, but every now and again memories come back so strong to him, that it upsets us both. On my return from Australia I had a short stop over in Singapore and I went to Changi prison and visited the museum and chapel, which my husband recalls so well. I also visited the many grave-yards, set out in vast areas of land; it brings it home to you just how many of our young men gave their tomorrow for our today, when you see all the thousands of graves there. We are very fortunate that my husband has remained as fit as he is, and has always done his best to keep going. He has always loved sport, and this might have helped him; however there are definite side effects which we feel relate to what he suffered. Please forward us a copy of the book, as I went to W.H. Smith's but they had sold out of them in just one day. We thank you for writing this book and for doing all you do to help our FEPOWs, as you know they are so often forgotten.

Yours sincerely,
Pamela Parker.

From Mrs. J. Jones, Leeds.......

Dear Mr. Bentinck,

I listened to your discussion with Bob Roberts the other night on BBC North which was most interesting and very moving. My brother who now lives in Adelaide S.A., was nineteen also when he was taken prisoner by the Japs. He was in the merchant navy and in January 1942 his ship, the Empress of Asia, carrying troops to Singapore, was attacked by Japanese aircraft. My brother was in the water for hours with the sharks, until an Australian ship picked them up and took them to Singapore. He also was sent to Changi prison when the Japanese invaded. My parents heard no news about him for eighteen months, until informed by the war office that he was believed to be a P.O.W. of the Japs in Changi. I was six years old when he returned home – it was a sight I will never forget. It is only these last few years when we have visited one another's homes, that he has told me about some of the ordeals of what he and his comrades went through. He has been back to changi with his wife and found it very moving indeed. I shall read your book with heart-ache, and sadness I know, but thanks for writing it. You should be proud of what you have done for your dads memory, and for what you are doing to help these brave, brave, men. Take care.

Yours sincerely,

Mrs. Joyce Jones.

From Mrs. B. Free, Wirral, Liverpool.......

Dear Sir,

Please forward me three copies of your book "MY DAD MY HERO". We heard you speaking on our radio Merseyside today with Linda whose programs we always find interesting. I know you must be so very proud to have had such a brave wonderful father; whilst my husband and I were around during the war we were not all that old to take part, but we would love our sons to own such a wonderful book, to show them what men gave for their today. Kindest regards to you and your wife, and all good wishes,

Sincerely,

Mrs. Brenda Free.

Letter from Mrs. J. Bell, Grimsby, Humberside........

Dear Mike,

Please forward me a copy of your book MY DAD MY HERO as soon as possible. It was so very interesting to hear you on our radio; also very moving. The dreadful things your poor father had to see and do at 19 years old must have damaged him for life. My father was killed in the war. I think it is wonderful that you have been able to raise a thousand pounds in just two months, and I hope you go from strength to strength. Your dad would be so proud of you. God bless.

Yours faithfully,

Mrs. Janet Bell.

Letter from Miss. A. Perman, London........

Dear Mr. Bentinck,

I recently heard you on radio and was very moved by the stories you told of your father's experiences during the second world war, as a Japanese prisoner of war. I am a woman of 33 years old, who did not lose anyone during the war. I feel such deep gratitude to men like your father – if it were not for people like him our lives would not be the same. I understand that the profits go to help these brave men still suffering these 50 years on. Please send me a copy of your book, and put the extra money towards your charity funds. Am I right in thinking you are writing another book of true stories, if so please retain my name and address to send me further details of when it will be ready. with all my good wishes and many thanks.

Miss Alison Perman.

Letter from Mr J. Ridley, Liverpool.......

Dear Mr. Bentinck,

Will you please forward my wife and I a copy of your book. We heard you on radio Merseyside talking to Linda Mc Dermott, and we sat in tears as it was so moving and true, for you see, I lost my two brothers in that nightmare –they were ALAN & FRANK GREGG always remembered. And also, please would you autograph the book for us. You may have noticed that ALAN & FRANKs names were Gregg – they were, in fact, my step brothers, but we were brought up like real "brothers", and two better brothers a man could never find. I have missed them so much throughout my life. I know I am not alone in saying this, for thousands of people are in the same boat as me, but what a waste of young lives it was, we pray that your efforts will go some way to making sure that these things never are allowed to happen again. Thank you for doing this for me, and the very best of luck with the book; I cant wait to read the next book as well.

Yours truly,
Jack Ridley.

Letter from M. McIntyre, Liverpool.......

Dear Mr. Bentinck,

I heard you on our Radio Merseyside, with Linda Mc Dermott. So very moving. I lost my sweetheart in that war in the Far East, as a prisoner of war. What a way to treat even prisoners. I could never find anyone to take his place; I kept comparing them to him and try as I may, they could never match up to him, so I never married – just gone through life with my memories of him deep in my heart. They have carried me through, and perhaps one day in that better place we shall be together at last. I thank you for your efforts in writing the book, as I know it could not have been easy for you, and must have brought a great deal of heartache to get it all together. It will be a lasting memorial to your dear father, who was a very brave man indeed, also even when he was suffering so much he still tried to care for others – such comradeship, they alone only know. The Hospital where the war trauma clinic is run here in Liverpool is the School of Medicine as I know you wanted to know about this. I trust your wife and yourself enjoyed your short stay in Liverpool and maybe you will be kind enough to come again, as I for one would love to hear you talk on the subject again and I'm sure I speak for all our Liverpool people. We get some bad press but as you say, we are good people and not as bad as we are made to sound. I have taken some knocks in life but my philosophy is it can only get better – yes, the Eternal optimist, that's me. Thank you for what you are doing to help our men; as you said on radio, they gave so much for us people should know what they suffered and endured for our today.

Yours most sincerely,
Margaret McIntyre.

From Mrs Clark, Oxford.......

Dear Mr. Bentinck,

I read your book and could not put it down until I had finished it – I cried, I smiled, and even laughed at the things your dad did as a youngster – thank God he had a good childhood, for he sure had his share of suffering at the hands of those little yellow men. My brother died on the death railway; I now know he was beaten to death by the camp guard gunzo; like your dad he was six feet tall and you know only to well how the guards hated the tall ones, for they had to look up to them. Let's hope your book is read by everyone then perhaps we can be sure it never happens again. I think Mr. Stephen Spielberg should make a film of it for the world to see. I thank you for all you and your wife are doing, and please let me know when that next book is ready and let me know when you are coming to Oxford to talk on our radio again as you are such a good speaker on the subject. God bless you and your wife – keep those books coming.

Yours sincerely,
Mrs Val Clark.

From Mr. L. Jackson, Bedfordshire.......

Dear Mike,

I heard you on our local BBC radio three counties talking to Simon Groom about your late father's suffering. I had to write to you to tell you that I was in some of the camps you mentioned, although it brought it all back to me I for one now feel better to talk about it. I lost my own dear brother, killed before my very eyes by those Japs and Korean guards, all because he spoke to a Thai near the camp fence, while trying to get some food for our boys in the sick hut, so don't ask me to forgive and forget. I thank you, Mike, for what you are doing for men like me. If only our Government felt like you about what we gave, then we might have got our compensation before we all die; I would imagine that's what all the governments say – keep leaving it then they will all be dead, and the problem will die with them. So thanks, Mike, for being that small fish in that vast ocean trying to swim against the tide to help us. Take care, all the best.

Yours thankfully,
Len. Jackson.

From Sue Humphery, Worcester.......

Dear Michael,

I heard you on radio Hereford and Worcester, talking to Jill Manley. After you had spoken for half an hour Jill finally spoke and told us all why you had spoken on for over half an hour – she could not speak for crying. I believed her as I sat listening crying as well. It was one of the best radio programs I have ever heard thanks to you. My own dear uncle was killed in the battle to save Singapore, and was therefore spared the horrific sufferings in the death railway camps. Perhaps at that time he was one of the lucky ones, but Michael, everyone should be made aware of what went on then. I can't wait to read "MY DAD MY HERO" and send you my very best wishes.

Sue Humphery.

From Mrs. J. Dewitt, Manchester.......

Dear Mr. Bentinck,

Please reserve me a copy of your book and any other books you write on this subject. The vile treatment of prisoners of war at the hands of those Japanese still turns my stomach; I feel bitterness having lost a dear cousin and friends through these scum, and I am happy knowing you are making yourself heard, for you speak so very well on the subject. I wish BBC GMR Manchester would have given you longer, as I for one could have listened all day about those stories of your brave dad and his mates. The things they did should not be swept under the carpet, as they have been for so long. If the Jews can constantly remind us, so should we for our dear boys were treated just as badly – beaten and starved to death. They say bitterness is like rust it eats away at you and at the heart, then so be it. That bomb should have wiped them out – the whole lot of them – for what they did. God does not pay his debts in money, lets hope he can forgive them for I cannot.

Sincerely,

Mrs. J. Dewitt.

Letter from Mrs. D. McCulloch, Cambridge.......

Dear Mr. Bentinck,

Having read the nice review of your book in the paper, I would like to have a copy please. My husband was your dad's Sergeant in the 1st Cambridgeshires, and I have a group photo of them taken at Galashiels, before they went abroad. My husband didn't go as after having embarkation leave, he was transferred to the Ordnance Corps then to the R.E.M.G. but I think working on the Gun steps in the radar huts at that time was the cause of him dying at a young age in 1959. When

The Cambridgeshire boys on camp before the war.

they all sailed from Liverpool, he was very upset, as they were all his friends even if he was their Sergeant, as he was with them in the Terries before the war. My husband was ordered to stay behind to attend the Court Marshals of the fourteen that did not turn up, but as we now know they were the lucky ones. The Court Marshals were held at Bury St Edmunds barracks. Thanks for your hard work in preparing the book and for your hard work to help these men – you can see why my family and I have such interest in the book.

Yours sincerely,

Dorothy McCulloch.

Sergeants' Mess 1st Battalion the Cambridgeshire Regiment at Galashiels, before they sailed to the Far East.

From Mr. P. Allanach, Leeds.......

Dear Mr Bentinck,

I am a long distance lorry driver. Last week I was north bound from Leeds via the M62 and up the M6 to Scotland when with luck I listened to BBC Radio Lancashire and heard you talking about your dear late father's suffering at the hands of those Japs. Slower and slower my truck went (now in Cumbria) as the signal became weaker and your harrowing tale saddening the core any man holds. If the signal becomes any weaker I'll have to pull onto the hard shoulder and fake a breakdown. I waited for the address or where I could obtain the book, and thank God managed to get it just before I was out of range. I decided at once that a copy of your book MY DAD MY HERO was a book I should read and a book my son should read. My son, Oliver, is only two and I am a mere 33 but I feel that we should never forget those men and women that gave their all for our freedom. I hold our war Veterans in the highest admiration – it's a shame the powers that be don't. We need to teach our young just what went on not just in Europe during the war, but above all the war in the Far East, where the Germans would have learnt more than a thing or two from the Japanese. I hope Oliver will one day sit down and read your book, just for him to take a moment of time to read what your father suffered and endured, and again suffered with for the rest of his life. If he can comprehend what your dad and his pals did for him, and us, then I for one shall see maybe some light to the cruelty. Sir, it is your writing that shall remind us all of those brave lads who humble the hardest of us.

I remain in your father's debt.

Phil Allanach. Leeds.

From Mrs. A. Drake, Newcastle upon Tyne.......

Dear Michael,

After hearing your moving story of your brave father's suffering, I think you should speak on behalf of these men for their compensation. I don't think any one could fail to be moved after hearing what you say about your dear dad – he would have been so proud of you. The Japs killed my young brother with a bayonet as he lay in a bed in Alexandra hospital after being wounded in the fighting; perhaps he lay in that other bed beside your dad. I have missed him so much all these years, that I could never forgive them for what they did to him. I am one of thousands who lost a loved

147

one, and I beg our Government to be strong and get our boys the compensation they so richly deserve. I can't wait to read the book, and I wish you every success with it. God bless you for what you are doing.

Yours thankfully,

Mrs. Alice Drake.

From Mr. R. Raikes, Sully, Nr. Cardiff, S. Wales.......

Dear Mike,

I am currently serving in Her Majesty's Royal Marines Commandos. In my career I have had a good experience of jungles, in the Far East, Malaysia etc. In that time I have also visited the Kwai memorial and graveyards in Thailand – I found it so very moving, to realise how many soldiers lay there and how many families are without the knowledge of their fate – for them there is no grave to visit, to place flowers on or to have a quiet moment in thought by their graveside as they are so many thousands of miles away. It goes without saying, Mike, that my colleagues and I are in full support of your charitable cause, and if there is anything or anyway we can help don't hesitate in dropping me a line.

Yours Faithfully,

Robert Raikes.

P.S. Please send the copies of the book as soon as possible, we cant wait to read it.

Dear Robert: Thank you for your letter and your kind offer of support. It warms my heart to know that kind caring young men like you are there for us today. I hope your career continues to be one of great success and happiness to you, and I hope and pray that you never have to see the kind of action and suffering that the men of the Welsh Regiments had to those 54 years ago. God bless you son.

Yours Thankfully, Mike Bentinck.

Letter from Mrs. Blaketon, Barrow-in-Furness, Cumbria.......

Dear Sir,

After hearing you on the Bob Roberts Programme last night, I could have listened to you talking of your dear fathers war time experiences for hours, as my biggest regret is that my own dear father did not talk to me about what he went through at the hands of the Japanese – he worked on the death railway. I know he lost his best mates out there, and know that this made it hard for him in life to make new friends. He suffered ill health for the rest of his life; thankfully he died suddenly of a heart attack when he was 64 years old. I say thankfully because at least he did not have to suffer any more. We in the family miss him so much, and all wish now that he could have spoken to us about those horrific things he went through. Please send two copies of your book MY DAD MY HERO for us to read, as we know it will help us to understand what our father went through. Also, as a daughter of an ex FEPOW, may I thank you for all you do to help these brave men. Yes, they are all *my* heroes too.

Yours most sincerely,

Mrs A. Blaketon.

Letter from Mr. G. Larson, Glasgow.......

Dear Michael,

I have read your book, and would just like to say how true to life at that time it was – I too was a Far Eastern prisoner of war, and was in a lot of the same camps as your father, I can remember one tall young British chap always receiving beatings, just because he was so tall; he was picked on because of his height as the Japs said he was not bowing enough to them – it might have even been your dad. I lost many friends in the camps, through cholera and dysentery, and two of them were beaten to death in front of me, because they were caught talking to some Thais, trying to get some food. I dug their graves, and buried them in the graveyard at Tamarkan, a thing I shall never forget, as they were my two best mates that I had grown up with. I still often sit and remember the fun we had at school together, and I will never forgive the Japanese for murdering them, for that is what they did to them – even though they begged for mercy, the Jap guards just beat them to death. Still, I must not burden you with it, but I must thank you for what you are doing to help us all; if only our government would follow your example, we might feel a bit better about what we gave to save our country, because heaven forbid if those Japs and them Germans had won the day, none of us would be here today. Keep up your good work, Michael. Never forget what your father shared with you, and thank you for sharing it with the rest of us.

Yours thankfully,

G. Larson.

Letter from Mrs. Weiss of Surrey.......

Dear Michael,

I listened very carefully to the story of your Father on London Talk-back last night. Tragically for so many years the mentally and physically tortured survivors could not talk, like your Father, with the result that in fact so little is known. It is not only the youth of Japan who have been fed on the glory of the emperor and the dropping of the bombs on Hiroshima and Nagasaki which are today a photographer's paradise. Maybe your book will right a terrible wrong.

On 11th June 1976 I sat alone in complete silence watching the screening of sketches made by Ronald Searle of St. Trinian's fame, as he observed and captured on precious scraps of paper. I remember.

My beloved husband - who perhaps shares a beer and a cigarette from time to time with your Father - escaped from Singapore on 13th February 1942, the day before the city fell, in a flotilla of around fifteen crowded vessels mostly unseaworthy. His companions and himself were the only ones in their dangerously listing junk to survive the onslaught which came at them from the skies. My Charles caught up with them in Burma.

At the end of a very long road, I now accept that we must all somehow live together but like you, I look at the older Japanese and wonder - I have twice visited Japan. I have no comment.

I think the Japanese should have representatives watching the Great March in August of this year, seeing all the veterans they did not crush. With their cars and their technology they now conquer but, please God, they will never kill the memories and the spirit of those who did not or just about made it.

A copy of your book, MY DAD, MY HERO please!

God bless you in your endeavours. Please include in your writings the few at that time who were human, like the guard with the bananas...as you did last night.

Very sincerely,
Lesley Weiss

Letter from Mrs G D Watt, Preston.......

Dear Michael,

Please forgive the informality – but I listened to your story on Radio Lancashire the other morning and was touched by your ex-POW's (rather, your father's) experiences during that awful time.

My husband was also a Far Eastern POW working on the infamous Burma-Siam railway and for 3 years his parents were not sure that he was alive. He was taken (with thousands of others) on 15th February '42 and spent some time in Changi before being shunted up-country to work in various Camps on the railway. He lost many good friends, having been in the Territorials prior to the war. He was a member of the Far Eastern POW Association, the Burma Star Association, and the Dunkirk Veterans Association. He got away from Dunkirk safely! and after spending a few months on the South Coast (awaiting the Germans who never came!) he was shipped out with his 88th Field Regiment R.A. to Singapore. He always said that he participated in the two great calamities of that war! Of course, Singapore was a complete tragedy for some and a blunder on the part of the "higher-ups "who planned it all. Those men were absolutely sacrificed!

You mentioned Billy Griffiths who we all know and who I have met personally on various occasions – I suppose you've read his book? I have also met Sir Edward Dunlop (then Col. Dunlop) the wonderful Australian surgeon who was loved by all the men in the various camps. He, of course, died a while ago and was accorded a State Funeral (almost) by his countrymen. What a pity the British Government don't think very much about our 1939-45 lads who never received such a thing as counselling – after a month or two of leave, they all went back to their occupations.

Gordon only talked freely about his imprisonment during the last few years of his life but his health was never the same again and he returned home a different man. I trust you will have time to read this letter, I just felt that I must write and let you know that some people understand .... or try to .... because anybody who was not there cannot possibly understand – even me!

Sincerely,

Joan Watt

PS. You DO know that some people who write about this era are inclined to get the dates wrong (see Lancashire Evening Post cutting opposite).

Singapore fell on the 15th February 1942 and our men fought on after all the VE Day celebrations in London! They had their lives saved by the dropping of the atomic bombs on the two Japanese cities later on – otherwise, the order was that they must all be 'exterminated' before the Japanese surrendered. I have many books on the subject including "The War Diaries of 'Weary' Dunlop "which he signed personally for us with a lovely inscription when we met him at a Conference.

We also attended a Luncheon at

Gordon David Watt, ex F.E.P.O.W. 88th Field Regiment, Royal Artillary.

Guildhall in London, hosted by the Lord Mayor and graced by the presence of Queen Elizabeth, the Queen Mother! – all very wonderful – but long overdue!!

Mrs. Watt also sent this cutting, she said he did not seek publicity - it was the the Lancashire Evening Post in September 1993 who *persuaded* him to be interviewed. Gordon lost all his hair but managed to keep his lovely teeth! He says (or said) that he attributed this to the 'seeded rice' they were fed which ruined their guts but polished their teeth! Sadly Gordon passed away in March 1994.

Gordon Watt

◯ GORDON Watt owes his life to an Australian surgeon who performed a tricky operation in a jungle hut.

There was no proper equipment or medicine, but without the bowel operation he would have died.

It was the memory of his parents back home which kept Gordon, 76, going as he too was forced into slave labour on Malayan jungle railways.

With barely enough food to keep him alive, his dreams were filled with thoughts of custard and huge platters of fried eggs.

Gordon had been a gunner with the Royal Artillery 88th Field Regiment when he was captured in Singapore in ~~August~~ 1942.
FEBRUARY

Amputated

Again, he suffered the range of tropical diseases, as well as from malnutrition and since his release has had numerous medical problems.

He said: "In one camp there was an awful problem with jungle ulcers and there were about 400 men with one or both legs missing because they had had to be amputated.

"The Japanese gave us nothing and the only reason we survived was because of our organisation. Indians and Malaysians taken to work on the railways perished in their thousands."

The veterans say they will be eternally grateful to the troops who broke through from Burma to liberate them and then went on to half rations to feed them.

Mrs. Elborn sent me this photograph and copy of a letter her husband sent their son in 1941.

Group photograph of Cambridgeshire A Company at Whittington Barracks, Litchfield, just before they sailed. Many of them were never to see England again. Jack Elborn (circled) is behind Jim Bentinck.

Private Elborn. J. No. 5932691.
1st. Cambs Regiment 'A' Company.
Whittington Barracks.
Lichfield. Staffs.

Dear Gerald,

I'm just writing a few lines for you, but as you are not quite old enough to read them you will have to ask your dear mother to do so. In a very short while now son, I shall be leaving my dear old England, to a land god knows where, so I am setting you a task which I know when you get a little older you will do. It is to look after your dear mother, and to see that no danger befalls her until I return home – she is a mother to be proud of, so don't play her up, or worry her too much. By my being on the road so much son, I have not seen much of you, but what I have seen of you I know that you are the greatest kid on earth, so don't forget to guard her, with your utmost ability, because I treasure her more than anything in the world. I must close now son, but I will write again soon, until then give mum a big kiss for me and give her all my love, which will stay in my heart forever.

Cheerio till later,

From your loving DAD John. xxxxxxxxxx

As you can see this is a letter sent by one loving father to his son before he sailed off to his unknown fate. After the war Mr. & Mrs. Elborn gave their love to fostering children, as this press cutting shows:

Just one big happy family!

RATHER a large number of children remember with affection Mrs Kathleen Elborn, who now lives in her third house in Whitehill Road. She has fostered 54 children.

Mrs Elbourn and her late husband, Jack who died two months ago, first lived at number 57. When they were asked to foster a family of four children, they could not accommodate them and moved to a four-bedroomed house at number 47.

However, when Mr Elbourn had a stroke 16 years ago, they decided to move to a smaller, more convenient house where Mrs Elbourn could look after him better.

Most of her large foster family keep in touch and some still call in to see her regularly.

During their spell of fostering, Mr Elborn walked four brides to their wedding to give them away.

Mrs Elbourn has two sons of her own, one born in 1940 and the other in 1960, and an adopted daughter.

Letter from Mrs. J. Button, Somerset.......

Dear Mr Bentinck,

Many thanks for your letter of 13 March together with the copy of the newspaper report, in response to my telephone call to order the book. I enclose a cheque for your book "MY DAD MY HERO" and will be pleased to receive it as soon as convenient.

I recall as a young girl of 17 being employed at Reading by the Army Records Office and whilst there many of the Japanese P.O.W.s came to us as a form of rehabilitation prior to returning to civvy street. At that time there was no indication of the deprivations they suffered and as youngsters they did not discuss anything with us as they were so shy (which we thought at the time, as we used to tease them) but since that time we found out the horrors they were put through, but did not want to recall.

My husband and I were moved greatly with your radio talk on Radio Bristol last Monday and we wanted to share your Father's book. We also look forward to your next book which you say will be ready in July.

Yours sincerely,

Mrs Jean Button.

S.S. Ormonde, the hospital ship that many of our brave lads came back on.

Our last letter is from Mrs. Doris M. Philips. who sent me a copy of the letter she sent to our Prime Minister:

Dear Prime Minister,

Having just returned from the Far East, where my late husband was a prisoner of war at the hands of the Japanese, whilst serving with the 5th Battalion of Suffolk Regiment and where he was a prisoner for 3 years.

As your constituency of Huntingdon is in Cambridgeshire, where many P.O.W/s were from, I thought you might be interested in my thoughts.

I was most fortunate to reside in a 5 star hotel where I had the benefit of air conditioning, a good comfortable bed, very good food and top medical assistance, while my husband and his colleagues were used as slave labour working under the most atrocious cruel camp guards, building the notorious Burma death railway, working some 12 to 18 hour days, cutting through solid rock, and swamp, and dense virgin jungle in a heat of 110+ degrees and in monsoon weather, on a ration of weevil infested rice, this being cooked in water from the river Kwai, as was the water they had to drink. This river was renowned for its filth and squalor. The rice ration was approximately 10 ounces a day if lucky but more times then not just six ounces. When I was ill from heat dehydration I was able to get the best help and all the modern drugs to prevent me from developing Cholera, beri, beri, dysentery and continual sickness all of which our men, plus many others, suffered without any help from their captors.

On my tour I visited several cemeteries with row upon row of graves, of young men whose age averaged 21 to 24 years old, most of them like my husband taken from their homes at the onset of war in 1939 and sent by the late Sir Winston Churchill to the Far East, knowing their fate was doomed before even landing, unlike troops who fought in the gulf war – that was the job they chose. After just two weeks I was able to come home, not like my dear husband and his comrades, who had to stay and be humiliated beyond belief. Like the few who survived my husband always thought himself most lucky to have been spared to come home, only to suffer daily mentally and physically with unseen pain and nightmares.

The war experiences took their toll and I lost a wonderful husband in October 92. The government showed their gratitude and awarded me a state pension of £65 per week. NO, Prime Minister, this is not from Hans Anderson's fairy tales, there are men from your constituency who could say to you "I KNOW BECAUSE I WAS THERE "Ask your Colleague, Sir Anthony Grant, my M.P. He told me in a letter that he was one of the first in to liberate these hell camps (just in case you think my imagination as ran away with me). Perhaps in the not to distant future you could get around to finding out about the large amount of money that the Japanese car factories owe this country in income tax as that would help repay the men that are left the compensation they deserve, as it will help them to pay the VAT on their fuel bills and the cost of living that seems to out jump all our little pensions, perhaps the Japanese will send us the 70,000+ Red Cross parcels that they never gave to our boys. I eagerly await your reply in extreme anticipation.

Yours faithfully,

Mrs Doris M. Philips, Foxton, Cambridge.

Dear Doris,

I'm sure you felt better after writing this letter to our Prime Minister – I just hope and pray like you that he will be strong and get our men the compensation they so richly deserve.

Well done Doris. Love Mike.

Well, my friends, we have now come to the end of our journey through this book.

I hope it has been a moving but worthwhile trip for you all. You have met all my HEROES, and have seen what they suffered for us all to be here today, we can never repay what they gave for our today as so many of you have said in your letters. I thank you all for writing to me and I would have loved to put all your letters into the book, but please believe me when I tell you that I can't thank you enough for buying my books for it is you that help me to be able to help my HEROES. Without your support I could not help them.

Watch out for that third book of true stories out next year, and until we meet again take care of yourself. God bless and keep you all safe.

Yours, Michael Bentinck

To all you kind people who ordered the book through our mail order, thank you for sending that bit extra to help these forgotten Heroes.

A TRIP TO JAPAN

Mr. CHARLES LYONS. Trip to Japan. And the day My war ended.

On our trip to Japan, Where we were treated like royalty, a man approached me and asked me which regiment I had belonged to. I replied that I had been in the royal Army Medical Corps. He said to me during the war he was a soldier in the Japanese army, fighting against the British in Burma. He had been badly wounded and captured, and taken prisoner, by the British, treated by the first aid station at the front and then removed to hospital. Upon recovery he was given light work around the prison camp. He had nothing but praise for the kindness shown to him from his captors. He said he did not know until two years ago how badly the British prisoners of war had been treated. He wished to apologise on behalf of the Japanese fighting soldiers. NOT THE PRISON CAMP GUARDS. For the way in which we were treated. In addition he would like to do anything he could to help us and would I do him the honour of shaking his hand.

IT WAS THEN THAT I FELT MY WAR HAD ENDED. for previously I had been extremely wary of going to Japan. We had always thought that we would never forgive and never forget, but now I have forgiven but not FORGOTTEN.

The End.